Porter Profiles

Jaguar D-type
The story of XKD 526

Porter Press International

©Porter Press International

All rights reserved. No part of this publication may be reproduced, stored in a retrieval system or transmitted, in any form or by any means, electronic, mechanical, photocopying, recording or otherwise, without prior permission in writing from the publisher.

First published in December 2019

978-1-907085-95-6

Published by
Porter Press International Ltd

Hilltop Farm, Knighton-on-Teme, Tenbury Wells, WR15 8LY, UK
Tel: +44 (0)1584 781588   Fax: +44 (0)1584 781630
sales@porterpress.co.uk
www.porterpress.co.uk

Edited by Simon Arron
Design & Layout by Martin Port

Printed by Gomer Press Ltd

COPYRIGHT

We have made every effort to trace and acknowledge copyright holders and we apologise in advance for any unintentional omission. We would be pleased to insert the appropriate acknowledgement in any subsequent edition.

Porter Profiles

Jaguar D-type
The story of XKD 526

John Elmgreen

Porter Press International

Also published by Porter Press International

The Jaguar Portfolio
Ultimate E-type – The Competition Cars
Jaguar E-type – The Definitive History (2nd edition)
Original Jaguar XK (3rd edition)
Jaguar Design – A Story of Style
Saving Jaguar

Exceptional Cars Series
No. 1 – Iso Bizzarrini – The remarkable history of A3/C 0222
No. 2 – Jaguar XK120 – The remarkable history of JWK 651
No. 3 – Ford GT40 MkII – The remarkable history of 1016
No. 4 – The First Three Shelby Cobras
No. 5 – Aston Martin Ulster – The remarkable history of CMC 614
No. 6 – Maseratti 4CLT – The remarkable history of chassis no. 1600
No. 7 – Ferrari 250 LM – The remarkable history of 6313

Great Cars Series
No. 1 – Jaguar Lightweight E-type – The autobiography of 4 WPD
No. 2 – Porsche 917 – The autobiography of 917-023
No. 3 – Jaguar D-type – The autobiography of XKD 504
No. 4 – Ferrari 250GT SWB – The autobiography of 2119 GT
No. 5 – Maserati 250F – The autobiography of 2528
No. 6 – ERA – The autobiography of R4D
No. 7 – Ferrari 250GTO – The autobiography of 4153 GT
No. 8 – Jaguar Lightweight E-type – The autobiography of 49 FXN
No. 9 – Jaguar C-type – The autobiography of XKC 051
No. 10 – Lotus 18 – The autobiography of Stirling Moss's '912'
No. 11 – Ford GT40 – The autobiography of 1075
No. 12 – Alfa Romeo Monza – The autobiography of the celebrated 2211130
No. 13 – Bugatti Type 50 – The autobiography of Bugatti's first Le Mans Car

De Luxe leather-bound, signed, limited editions with slipcases are available for most titles.
Books available from retailers or signed copies direct from the publisher.
To order simply phone +44 (0)1584 781588, fax +44 (0)1584 781630,
visit the website or email sales@porterpress.co.uk

Keep up-to-date with news about current books and new releases at:
www.porterpress.co.uk

Contents

Introduction		7
1	The Production D-type is announced	8
2	The Anderson/Pitt era, 1856–1959	16
3	Frank Matich & Leaton Motors, 1959–1961	38
4	Racing Winds Down, 1965–1967	54
5	A Long Love Affair, 1967–2014	56
6	Back to the UK, 2014	64
7	XKD 526 in Detail	68
Index		94

Acknowledgements

The drivers involved in racing Jaguar D-type XKD 526 in the 1950s and early 1960s are sadly deceased. Before the losses of Geordie Anderson and Bill Pitt in particular, however, Brisbane-based Les Hughes of *Jaguar Magazine* was able, over the years, to put together much information about the car's early days. His work in that regard has been a most valuable resource.

Terry McGrath was most helpful, particularly in relation to various details of the car's history and in providing most of the photographs included here.

Bill Colyer was one of the tradesmen involved in the more or less simultaneous rebuild of XKD 526 and XKD 510, in Sydney during the late 1970s and early 1980s. A Qantas sheet metal worker, chosen for his expertise with aluminium and riveting, he supplied many details of how, in his spare time, he brought these cars back together.

Keith Berryman owned XKD 526 for some 48 years and was most helpful in recounting this long-standing relationship. This began as a schoolboy, when he visited Melbourne's Albert Park circuit in November 1956 and saw the car for the first time. Little did he know that one day it would be his! The story of its restoration many years later bordered on the epic.

Chris Keith-Lucas only came into contact with the car in 2014, when he was sent from the UK to Australia on a quick inspection mission (book-ended by two very long flights) as Keith Berryman offered it for sale. His comments on what he saw on that occasion – and more so on what he was subsequently able to find when he was entrusted with looking after the car back in the UK – were fascinating. These included his acknowledgement of original components still fitted to the car. Such things are so rarely reliably recorded in the course of a car's life and remain to be discovered only during the most intimate of inspections – which Chris certainly carried out. He was able to work out which parts of the car had been rebuilt during the Australian restoration and which original mechanical components had remained throughout its life. Appropriate improvements followed.

Others who contributed their recollections include Steve Sulis and Paul Cummins, son of Jaguar specialist Ian. The assistance of the staff at the State Library of New South Wales, where many dozens of hours were spent trawling through numerous period motoring publications, was much appreciated. Thanks also to the many motoring journalists who recorded the details of the racing events and some related background in the journals of the day.

Finally, many thanks are due to Philip Porter and the staff at Porter Press International for the opportunity to compile this history, and for having applied their considerable skills and experience to bring the whole project together.

Introduction

The D-type made its first Le Mans appearance in June 1954 and that October Jaguar announced that it would produce the model for customers, displaying a works car at the Earls Court Motor Show later in the month. The marque's successes at Le Mans had forged its reputation for building cars that were not just beautiful but also fast and reliable. As renowned Jaguar historian Andrew Whyte wrote: "From the outset, to own a D-type Jaguar was the dream of many a racing driver."

In the 1950s, Australia was a solid market for Jaguar (although like almost everywhere else, it paled in comparison with North America). Jaguar's Brisbane distributor, the company of Cyril and Doris 'Geordie' Anderson, already had a background in motor racing through the exploits of Geordie in an XK 120 OTS and Geordie and Bill Pitt in the XK 120 FHC with which they won the 24-hour race held at Mt Druitt, near Sydney, in 1954. Cyril was highly successful in business, mainly importing trucks. The Andersons were among those who tried to get their hands on a D-type at an early date.

For Jaguar, of course, the D-type was primarily a competition car. Making chassis available to private owners could not take priority over the factory's effort to achieve success at Le Mans. As a result, it was not until August 1955 that the first of the so-called production D-types was delivered to a private customer. These cars were based on the 1954 design, so were already a year out of date in competitive terms. That month, Jaguar would reduce its proposed total production of D-types from 100 cars to 67. Andrew Whyte added: "As might be imagined, the situation began with a stream of 'serious' enquiries in 1954 and 1955, petering out as the 1956 season progressed, and ending with a surplus of obsolescent machines in the following winter." A price increase had not helped.

The works and Ecurie Ecosse cars were a different story and the D-type continued to achieve major successes for another couple of years as a result of continuous development.

In Australia, factory preparation or even highly funded racing development was scarce or non-existent, so the arrival of the production D-type was eagerly awaited. Finally receiving their car in December 1955, the Andersons wasted no time in raising the marque's profile locally. They put the car into action in sprints early in 1956 – with suitable local publicity focusing initially on Geordie's 'need for speed' as a housewife, and mother of six. Later in the year, the Andersons were to become much more serious in competition, with the car in the hands of Bill Pitt. He raced it with success before it passed to Leaton Motors and highly capable drivers Frank Matich, Doug Chivas and Barry Topen. It even acquired a hard top that enabled Matich to win an Australian GT Championship in 1961. An accident early in '62 brought its serious racing career to an end.

The D-type then languished for a period, taking part in just the occasional minor event – although it did win the inaugural Tom Sulman Trophy race for historic cars in 1970. In its later years, after a local rebuild finished in the early 1980s, it regularly graced major motorsport events in Australia as a symbol of Jaguar's wonderful 1950s racing heritage. The car returned to the UK in 2015, following which Chris Keith-Lucas was able to conduct what, for want of a better term, might be called an exercise in industrial archaeology, and was pleased with what he found. The car has benefited greatly from his expertise and preparation and, after various improvements, it is wonderful to know that it has again been seen in action.

XKD 526 raced more than 50 times in Australia and had one of the longest periods of single ownership for any D-type. Despite its lengthy career, and a few hefty mishaps along the way, it has been found to retain a high degree of originality. Short histories of this car have been written before, but this is a more comprehensive story of its long life Down Under and subsequent return home.

John Elmgreen, Sydney, November 2019

Chapter One

The production D-type is announced

Jaguar introduced the XK 120 Super Sports model to the world at the London Motor Show in October 1948, regarding it as a showcase for a new twin overhead-cam engine that was primarily destined for its saloon range. But its latest saloon, the Mk VII, was not quite ready.

The XK 120 was subsequently found to live up to a claimed top speed that matched its name – 120mph – and, less than two years after its somewhat tentative introduction, was entered for the 1950 Le Mans. It performed creditably enough for Jaguar to decide that a specially developed competition version might just be able to win the event. The XK 120C – the C-type – was born and duly achieved that victory in 1951. After a disastrous 1952, when all three works C-types failed to finish the endurance classic, Jaguar won again in 1953 and the C-type duly made way for the D-type, which won Le Mans in 1955, 1956 and 1957.

Australia was lacking, however, when it came to teams with factory support, or significant funding of any kind, while top-class circuits were also in short supply.

The opportunity for a few members of the public to acquire a cutting-edge Jaguar sports

The production D-type was announced by Jaguar on 4 October 1954, and this photo was taken at Earl's Court in London the day before the British International Motor Show opened there on 20 October 1954, where the car was displayed. It was not a production D-type but chassis XKD406, the last of the 1954 works cars, raced by the works just once (at Dundrod in September).
Getty Images

The production D-type is announced

racer arose when the company began building its so-called 'production' D-types in 1955 and through into 1956.

In 1954, just five D-types were built as works cars. The following year an additional eight works and designated racing team cars were built and production of a further 67 cars was initiated for outside customers. These had chassis numbers from XKD 501 to XKD 575 and met a variety of fates. Jaguar sold 42 such cars, 18 to the USA, 10 to the UK, three to Australia, two to France and one to each of nine other countries. Of the remaining 25, nine were either destroyed during a factory fire in February 1957 or dismantled, while 16 became XKSSs. In 1956 there was a final batch of six new 'long-nose' D-types, all of them built as works cars. XKD 526 was one of the three cars sold new to Australia.

By 1955 there had already existed a strong relationship between the Australian distributors and the factory, which allocated a new D-type to Brisbane dealership Westco, run by the Anderson family that had been appointed Jaguar agents in 1947, operating from 122 Margaret Street.

Of the three production D-types sent to Australia, XKD 526 was the first. It had no

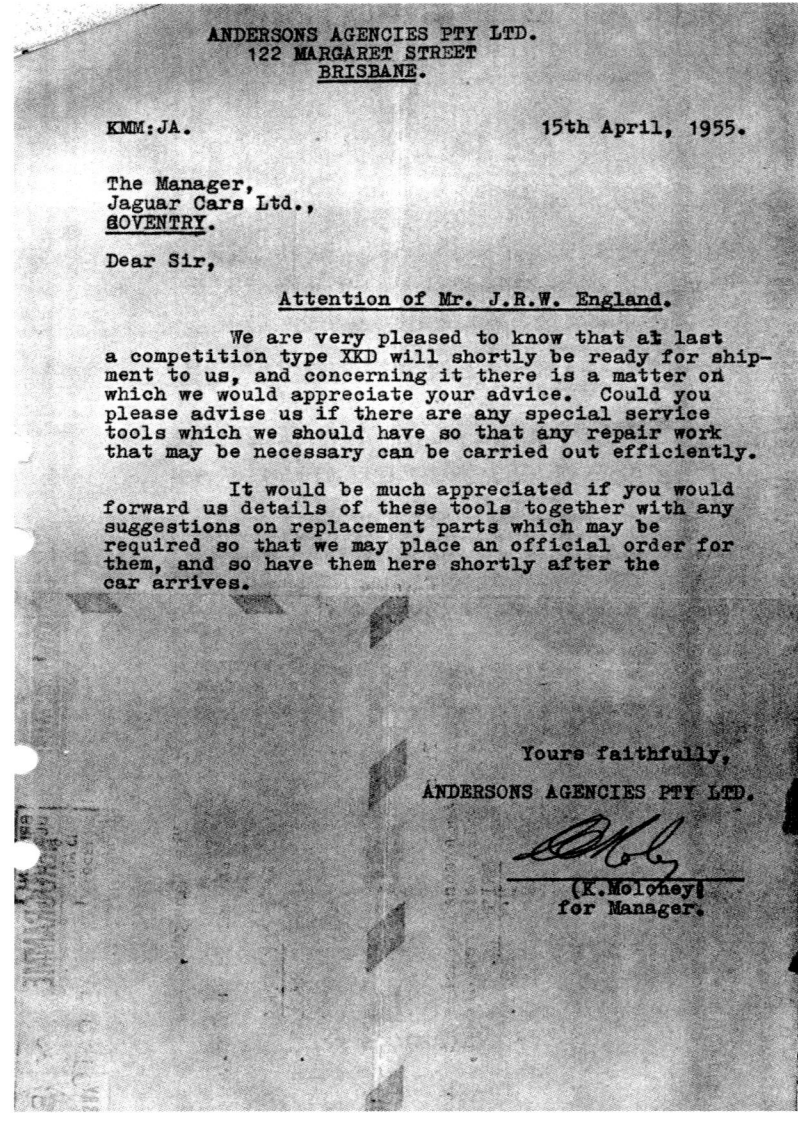

The Andersons had ordered their D-type some months earlier and in April 1955 were pleased to learn their car would "shortly" be available – although it would be a further six months before it was shipped. This was the case with many 'production' D-types, resulting in cancelled orders for what was fast becoming an out-of-date sports racing car. In August 1955 Jaguar reduced its proposed total production of D-types from 100 cars to 67.
Terry McGrath Motoring Archives

Les Bottrill, who tested all of the production D-types, gave XKD 526 its second run (110 miles) at MIRA on 28 September 1955, having previously done 211 miles in the car in its first test at the same venue three weeks beforehand.
Terry McGrath Motoring Archives

The production D-type is announced

Geordie Anderson set for a day's racing in Queensland in her aluminium XK 120 chassis number 660015
Terry McGrath Motoring Archives

XKD 520 & XKD 532

XKD 526 was one of three D-types exported to Australia as new cars. The others were XKD 520 and XKD 532. The former was dispatched from the works in December 1955, in time to compete at Albert Park, Melbourne, on 11 March 1956. It raced initially in the hands of Bib Stillwell and was owned for a short period in 1957 by one of Australia's best known radio and TV stars, Jack Davey. That was a concern to his management, as Davey was not known for restraint with cars, though one of his friends was at the helm when it was very badly smashed in a road accident. The wreck went to leading racer Frank Gardner and was rebuilt to resume competition. It was later used by David Finch before returning to the UK in 1967 and passing into the hands of former Jaguar apprentice Richard Attwood, by then a well-known driver. Several others have owned it since.

XKD 532 left the works in October 1956 and reached customer Jack Parker in Sydney by March 1957. It was raced locally by Jack Murray (1958-1961) and was subsequently acquired by businessman Bob Jane, who had competed successfully in Jaguar saloons and a lightweight E-type but did not race the D-type. In 1976 it was on display in a Sydney showroom when it was stolen and crashed. It was then rebuilt before returning to England in 1988.

recorded build date but was dispatched on 13 October 1955 to be shipped via Liverpool to Brisbane. It was fitted with engine number E2042-9, body number 2026 and painted British Racing Green with a tan interior. The gearbox number is not recorded, but GBD134 is likely.

XKD 520 arrived in Australia circa March 1956 and XKD 532 reached Sydney about a year later and of the three D-types sold new in Australia, XKD 526

Doris 'Geordie' Anderson

By all accounts, 'Geordie' Anderson (1908-1995) was a remarkable lady. She was born in Scotland, despite her adopted name, and arrived penniless in Australia as a child with her parents and sister Kush. She married former international motorcycle racer Cyril Anderson, who was also later involved in car racing. The Anderson family's early success was based on their transport business and in 1947 Andersons Agencies was appointed Jaguar distributor for Queensland and the Northern Territory. The company also traded under the name of Westco.

Softly spoken 'Geordie' raised a large family before she turned to motor racing with the 15th RHD XK 120 built. This car, completed in November 1948, arrived in Australia in early 1950. It was used by the Andersons at a number of race meetings between August 1950 and September 1952. The car (presumed driven by Mrs Anderson) was recorded at 124.5mph at a sprint meeting at Leyburn in April '52, breaking the state speed record.

Subsequently she teamed up with Bill Pitt, who had closed his own business to take a senior role with Westco, to race the 15th RHD XK 120 fixed-head coupé built and

After the aluminium XK 120 was burnt in a workshop fire, the Andersons took delivery of a specially prepared XK 120 FHC, coincidentally also chassis number 15, which Geordie raced and hill climbed on a number of occasions.
Terry McGrath Motoring Archives

Geordie Anderson topping up the radiator of the aluminium XK 120 660015 with a water bag, a popular item hung on the front of cars in Australia in the 1940s – 1960s.
Terry McGrath Motoring Archives

The production D-type is announced

win the first 24-hour race staged in Australia.

'Probably the highlight of the XK days,' wrote the eminent Jaguar historian Andrew Whyte of this period in Australian Jaguar history in his book *Jaguar Sports Racing & Works Competition Cars to 1953*, 'was Mrs 'Geordie' Anderson's victory in the Mount Druitt 24-hour race in February 1954, which she won in an XK 120 fixed-head coupé, assisted by Bill Pitt and Charles Swinburne.' They defeated a large field including Peter Whitehead and Tony Gaze in the former's C-type, XKC 039 which led but retired.

Perhaps her greatest triumph though was to finish seventh outright, with Bill Pitt, in the 10,000-mile 1957 Around Australia Trial driving an automatic Jaguar Mk VIII - behind six VWs!

She and Pitt won a number of trophies including first automatic and first place for a large car, and 'Geordie' took the Ladies Trophy.

She is described by Les Hughes, Jaguar historian and Editor of the *Australian Jaguar Magazine*, as a very petite and modest lady, who later in her life was happily reunited with Bill Pitt and the D-type. He states that, at the time of her death, the Anderson family was one of the wealthiest in Australia, and she was very proud of her Jaguar connection.

Geordie at the wheel of the Mk VIII in which she, Bill Pitt and Jim Abercrombie competed in the 1957 Mobilgas Rally, a 10,500 mile 'Around Australia' event. There is no record of her competing in the works prepared Mk I later driven with great success by Bill Pitt.
Terry McGrath Motoring Archives

remained there the longest. Keith Berryman had the car from 1967 to 2015 – one of the longest continuous private ownerships of a D-type anywhere in the world.

Other D-types to have frequented Australia are XKD 510 (Hallihan, Cummins, Haigh, Daly – 1967-1982, 1988 onwards), XKD 540 (converted to an XKSS but retaining its D-type chassis number - O'Neill, Ralph, Hyams, Clemens – 1962-1972) and XKD 545 (Briggs – 1980-2002).

Les Hughes records that XKD 526 was in fact owned in one-third shares by Cyril and Doris (aka 'Geordie') Anderson, Bill Pitt and Charles Swinburne. The car was commonly mentioned in race programmes as entered by Geordie Anderson and driven by Bill Pitt.

Geordie Anderson (1908-1995) was regarded as a remarkable

In 1954, the team of Bill Pitt, Geordie Anderson and Charlie Swinburne won the 1954 24 hour race at Mt Druitt, just outside Sydney, seeing off such opposition as a works C-type Jaguar in the hands of Peter Whitehead, a driver who had won for Jaguar at Le Mans in 1951. Unfortunately, Geordie crashed this car heavily at the 1954 Australian Grand Prix.
Terry McGrath Motoring Archives

Porter Profiles – Jaguar D-type • XKD 526

The original press caption read 'D-TYPE DOWN UNDER: happy lady in her newly acquired Jaguar D type is Mrs Cyril Anderson of Brisbane, Australia. She plans to race it in suitable events there this season.'
Terry McGrath Motoring Archives

The production D-type is announced

XKD 526 is believed to have been exhibited at the 1956 Brisbane Motor Show and was certainly put to good use on display at the Andersons' own premises. Terry McGrath Motoring Archives

woman, taking to motor racing in her early 40s in XK 120s after having raised six children. She was to become the first and perhaps only woman to race a D-type as a new car? The Australian press certainly picked up on her ownership. She was described as a 'housewife' but at the same time also holder of the Australian women's land speed record. She was quoted thus, 'I'll use the Jag mainly for racing, but sometimes it will come in handy as a "hack" for doing the shopping.'

Shortly after the arrival of the D-type, Charles Swinburne became very ill with cancer and sold his share to the others.

Bill Pitt

Bill Pitt (1926-2017) raced XKD 526 extensively. He was born in Brisbane and had been in the Australian Navy during the Second World War. He became active in motorsport from 1948 and later ran LPS Motors, a garage business in Brisbane, with Charles Swinburne and Ray Lewis. A common interest in motorsport led Cyril Anderson to invite Pitt and Swinburn to share his XK120 FHC in a 24-hour race at Mount Druitt, near Sydney, on 31 January 1954. They won after Peter Whitehead's C-type (shared with Tony Gaze and Alf Barrett) dropped out when the rough track surface caused suspension damage. In 1957 Pitt, Geordie Anderson and Jimmy Abercrombie drove an automatic Jaguar Mk VIII in the Mobilgas Around Australia Trial and, in an event that only about half the starters completed, were beaten only by half a dozen Volkswagens. Pitt regarded this as his most satisfying motorsport performance. After his efforts with the D-type, Bill moved on to racing a 3.4-litre Jaguar Mk1 saloon with great success, winning the 1961 Australian Touring Car Championship.

After retiring from competition the following year, he devoted much of his time to motorsport administration. He was a modest individual, universally regarded as a gentleman by those who knew him well.

Bill Pitt in the works prepared Jaguar Mk I (second version) with his usual race number #34. The car survives in very original condition in Australia. Terry McGrath Motoring Archives

Chapter Two
The Anderson/Pitt era
1956-1959

The car's early competitive appearances were local to Brisbane. Strathpine was a venue set up on an old Second World War airstrip, about 12 miles north of the city. The car made its first public appearance at speed here on 30 January 1956, when it was driven by Geordie Anderson over a flying quarter-mile. It had just half a mile 'wind-up', 300 yards in which to stop and clocked 120mph in third gear – a record.

At the Leyburn sprints on 19 February 1956 she recorded a state record speed of 135.2mph for the flying quarter – despite a headwind. She had previously held the same record in her XK 120 open two-seater and her XK 120 fixed-head coupé. She had the car out for a third time at Strathpine on 17 March 1956, but no results are available.

It was entered on 8 April 1956 at Lowood, a flat, safe venue about 50 miles west of Brisbane and another wartime fighter base, shortly to become Queensland's premier motorsport venue. Anderson ran the car in the three-lap sports and saloon scratch race, finishing second behind an Austin Healey 100S, and in the four-lap Champions Scratch Race, taking third behind Arthur Griffiths's HWM Jaguar and Charles Whatmore's Jaguar Special.

The track at Leyburn was obviously too short and the surface would best be described as 'loose gravel'.
Terry McGrath Motoring Archives

Having previously raced her XK120 OTS and XK120 FHC, there was a sense of inevitability that Geordie Anderson would race the D-type.
Terry McGrath Motoring Archives

The Anderson/Pitt era, 1956-1959

XKD 526 with the front taped up to stop the worst of the damage from the loose shale surface at Strathpine. Behind is the Whatmore Jaguar Special, a Standard 14 chassis fitted with a Mk VII engine and a pair of H8 carburettors.
Terry McGrath Motoring Archives

Thereafter it would be Bill Pitt (1926-2017) who raced the car extensively. His performances with XKD 526 – and thereafter with Jaguar saloons – led respected author Barry Green to rate him as 'the top Queensland driver of the 1950s'.

Pitt got his first competitive drive at Lowood on 12 August 1956, when he won the Champions Scratch Race and set the fastest time on his way to fourth place in the Sports and Saloon Car Handicap. Each race lasted four laps and Pitt established a new track record.

After the local shakedowns in Queensland, things became far more serious when Pitt took the car south to Bathurst, New South Wales, where racing was staged on Sunday 30 September and Monday 1 October 1956 (Labour

The Anderson/Pitt era, 1956-1959

Day holiday) at the NSW Road Racing Championship meeting. On a very cold, windy weekend, the fields assembled were as good as the state had ever known.

Bib Stillwell was there in XKD 520, the D-types looking almost identical in BRG. They did not run against each other, however, as Pitt opted to compete with the racing cars and Stillwell with the sports cars.

Pitt finished second to Stan Jones (father of Alan) in a new Maserati 250F grand prix car in both a three-lap scratch race and the main 100-mile (26-lap) NSW Road Racing Championship event, ahead of the locally built Jaguar Specials of Jack Robinson and Jack Neal, among others. In that feature race, Jones won by more than seven-and-a-half minutes.

Bill Pitt adding some fuel at Lowood in 1956. Again, the front was taped up to prevent stone chips from the loose gravel surface.
Terry McGrath Motoring Archives

QRDC Presents
QUEENSLAND RACING DRIVERS' CLUB LTD.

1956 LOWOOD AUGUST MOTOR RACE MEETING

AT
LOWOOD, SUNDAY, 12th AUGUST, 1956

Held under the International Sporting Code of the F.I.A. and the Competition Rules of the Confederation of Australian Motor Sport.

SOUVENIR PROGRAMMES : 1/-

The Anderson/Pitt era, 1956–1959

Bathurst: 'Bib' Stillwell in XKD 520 #90 and Bill Pitt in XKD 526 #9 head down the mountain onto Conrod Straight on the Grand Parade display lap at 11am. Behind is #14, the Jack Robinson Special that was based on an XK120 and had a great Australian race history in its own right. Terry McGrath Motoring Archives

A spectator trying XKD 526 for size at Bathurst. The noted Pritchett special, 'Monster', with a supercharged Mercedes engine in a Crossley chassis, is in the background.
Terry McGrath Motoring Archives

Lowood, 4 November 1956
The D-types finally met in combat in Queensland, at the Lowood Courier-Mail Tourist Trophy event. As *Modern Motor* described it, Stillwell had so far 'reigned supreme'. But Lowood was Pitt's home turf.

The main event was the Queensland Tourist Trophy, the first TT event to be held in Queensland. It was of one-hour duration, with a Le Mans-type running start and one compulsory pit stop.

Pitt won with Stillwell second, 28s in arrears – despite the leader having run the whole race with only third and fourth gears, according to period press reports. Leaving aside tyre and gearbox problems, however, the cars were evidently evenly matched, as both had equalled the lap record and it appeared that Stillwell had held back somewhat, particularly early in the race. Stillwell was also timed at 150mph through the flying quarter, just ahead of Pitt's fastest.

'Pitt won with Stillwell second, 28s in arrears – despite the leader having run the whole race with only third and fourth gears'

Albert Park, 25 November & 2 December 1956

Melbourne hosted the 1956 Olympic Games, which took place from 22 November to 8 December – the first time they had been held in the Southern Hemisphere. During that period, the first Australian Tourist Trophy and the 21st Australian Grand Prix took place at Albert Park, over consecutive weekends.

These were significant. As Barry Green wrote: 'Here, for the first time, we had a current works Formula 1 and sports car team and other leading international drivers in ex-factory racers.' Officine Alfieri Maserati took part with Stirling Moss and Jean Behra, each in a 300S, while Peter Whitehead and Reg Parnell (Super Squalo Ferraris) and Ken Wharton (Maserati) also made the trip. Fields of such international calibre were regarded as the best that had yet been assembled in Australia.

Both D-types were on the front row at Albert Park, with some 32 cars on the grid. Stillwell in XKD 520 on the left led Pitt in XKD 526, but the latter's race was soon to end when he came to grief at Melford Corner. Terry McGrath Motoring Archives

The Anderson/Pitt era, 1956-1959

In the main event on the first weekend, Pitt and Stillwell drove their D-types in a 32-lap, 100-mile race. While Pitt had home advantage earlier in the month at Lowood, unlike Stilwell he was a newcomer to Albert Park. The Maseratis of Moss and Behra were predictably dominant, finishing a lap ahead of Wharton and two clear of the locals in fourth and fifth. Pitt steadily improved his lap times as he got used to the circuit, but Stillwell led him until the race's closing stages, when his engine faltered, began to emit smoke and caused him to drop behind Pitt.

The following weekend, a reported crowd of 100,000 turned out to watch. The Argus Trophy (eight laps, 25 miles) for sports cars was run as a curtain-raiser to the Australian Grand Prix.

Both D-types were on the front row in a 32-car field. Stillwell led Pitt down the main straight on lap one, but as the pack neared its end, they were (as *Australian Motor Sports* recounted), 'confronted very quickly with the problem of getting 32 cars through a hole wide enough for four, at most, at Melford Corner [named after a local Ford dealer]. Bill Pitt failed to survive this problem, entering the corner a good 20 mph too

Bill Pitt failed to take Melford Corner at Albert Park on 2 December 1956 and finished upside down among the hay bales. The accident was also captured on movie film.
Terry McGrath Motoring Archives

Porter Profiles – Jaguar D-type • XKD 526

The Anderson/Pitt era, 1956-1959

At the start of the racing activities, American oil company Mobilgas organised some publicity photographs of various cars which included the Cooper Jaguar and XKD526. Bill Pitt stands to the right of the car, hands in pockets.
Terry McGrath Motoring Archives

Photograph taken by schoolboy Keith Berryman – later owner of this car – at Albert Park, November 1956. Keith Berryman

fast in his anxiety to make it first, with the result that he lost the D-type and overturned it on the straw bales, where it decided to add to the excitement by setting light to itself. Bill was unhurt, the fire was quickly put out and the D-type bodily carried off the course…' The car had ended up both upside-down and travelling backwards. Numerous cars passed the inverted car, including at least two on the inside, between the D-type and the straw bales. The marshals were amazed, having extinguished the fire and righted the car, to find Bill was not underneath. He had been thrown out and survived virtually unscathed.

The race, of course, continued, Stillwell in his D-type continuing to lead until being passed by eventual winner Jack Brabham (Cooper-Climax). Stillwell was not far behind in second.

In the 250-mile Australian Grand Prix, Moss and Behra again finished first and second in their Maserati 250Fs, in a class of their own.

Keith Berryman, who was later to own XKD 526 for 48 years, later recalled: 'I was going to school in Albury when it [the D-type] first came out, and I went down to Albert Park to see it race. I've still got the picture I took of Bill Pitt sitting in it.'

XKD 526 was trailered back to Brisbane for repairs. In due course, the bonnet re-emerged with a slightly different shape to its mouth, now slightly bigger and more rectangular. The car was also repainted bronze.

During the course of the car's rebuild, it appears that Pitt and the Andersons took the opportunity to check the state of the car's mechanicals and were in touch with the factory about some service items. Jaguar supplied new parts – which evidently included a ZF limited slip differential. Jaguar also sent to Brisbane a heavier anti-roll bar for the front suspension, plus one for the rear links (these had been upgrades introduced in March 1956), together with a full-flow oil filter (a modification made due to some experiences of bearing failure from dirty oil) and other parts. Pitt also fitted a new gearbox.

The D-type had a braking quirk that Pitt described as follows: 'At Bathurst, at the bottom of Conrod [the long

straight], you'd need three to five pumps to get brakes. Jimmy [the Andersons' mechanic] worked out we were getting shake-back of the disc pads. They would be all right on a perfect surface, but on a rough road they would get shaken away from the disc and, of course, there were so many pads that just a small shake-back displaced a lot of fluid. Jimmy fitted a line pressure valve that kept a residual pressure in the system, and that worked very well. We rang "Lofty" England about the problem, and they denied any experience of it. But they later fitted the same sort of thing, which gave me great satisfaction.'

Albert Park, 17 & 24 March 1957

The car returned to competition three months later on 17 March 1957 at Albert Park in Melbourne, in the Victorian Tourist Trophy at the Moomba meeting – an event that had little chance of matching the excitement a few months beforehand, when Stirling Moss and other international stars had appeared.

AMS reported that XKD 526 was 'beautifully restored' and looked 'outstanding in burnished bronze duco'.

On the first day, in the 100-mile (32-lap) Tourist Trophy,

XKD 526 now on the front row of the grid for the Victorian Tourist Trophy, alongside the Maserati 300S (chassis 3055) of Doug Whiteford and the Aston Martin DB3S #103 of Tom Sulman. Terry McGrath Motoring Archives

The Anderson/Pitt era, 1956-1959

it looked as if Doug Whiteford – driving the ex-Behra Maserati 300S that had competed in the Olympic meeting late the previous year – would dominate. That he did, running untroubled to win by about 30s from the equally solitary Pitt.

One weekend later, at the same venue, Pitt offered Bib Stillwell a chance to drive the unmistakable 'burnished' D-type in the sports car scratch race (25 laps). He finished third, behind Whiteford.

Pitt took the car back for the 10-mile Victorian Trophy Handicap for sports and racing cars and finished sixth from the third row of the grid, the cars ahead including Lex Davison's winning Ferrari 500/625, Brabham's Cooper and Whiteford's Maserati.

XKD 526 as it appeared in bronze at Albert Park in March 1957, repaired after its crash the previous December. The Jaguar transfer on the nose of the bonnet was now gone and an XK 120 badge had been fitted. Terry McGrath Motoring Archives

XKD 526, now in bronze and sporting the XK 120 bonnet badge. Terry McGrath Motoring Archives

The Anderson/Pitt era, 1956-1959

Track surfaces in Queensland were far from optimal, resulting in major tyre wear. Terry McGrath Motoring Archives

An English visitor's view

In July 1957, experienced English racer and enthusiast James Abbott spent some time in Australia and wrote: 'Australia has established a motor racing tradition that reaches around the world. The great Australian reliability trials are reported in the British daily newspapers at length; drivers such as Brabham are well known to English enthusiasts; Australian-built cars like the Ausca and the Maybach have proved to the world that this country has both the technical skill and engineering knowledge to turn out machines capable of holding their own in any company. The Albert Park circuit, situated in the middle of Melbourne, is undoubtedly one of the finest road racing circuits in the world and is the envy of London racing enthusiasts, who have nothing to compare with it and have to travel many miles to and from their day's motor racing.'

Lowood, 7 April & 16 June 1957

Bill Pitt was back in the D-type at Lowood, not long after the track had been remodelled.

The meeting marked the first appearance of a Porsche Spyder in Queensland and *Sports Car World* noted that Pitt was out to 'show the crowd the Jaguar's supremacy over the Spyder'. This he did most emphatically, overcoming some tyre difficulties to take victory and lower his own lap record by three seconds.

Back at the same venue two months later, the Queensland Road Racing Championship was run in the format of two nine-lap heats and a 20-lap final, before a 15,000-strong crowd.

Frank Gardner was entered in C-type XKC 037, although neither he nor Pitt could expect to match Lex Davison's Super Squalo Ferrari or Stan Jones's Maserati. But the latter withdrew from the final with mechanical problems, having won its heat.

Davison had no real challengers, smashing the old lap record by seven seconds, and Pitt finished third behind him and the Cooper-Holden of Tom Hawkes. The D-type had needed a pit stop to change a tyre and several other cars retired from the race. Gardner's C-type was fifth, on this occasion a full lap behind Pitt.

The Anderson/Pitt era, 1956-1959

Bathurst, 6 October 1957
By the time Bathurst came around, the Pitt D-type was back in dark green.

The main event, the 26-lap/100-mile New South Wales Championship for Racing Cars, was won by Lex Davison.

In the 13-lap NSW Championship for Sports Cars, Pitt was third behind winner David McKay at the helm of the ex-Moss/Collins Aston Martin DB3S (DB3S9), which had raced at Le Mans the previous year. The Aston lapped a striking six seconds faster than the D-type – proof, not that it was needed, of the benefit of works preparation. McKay recorded 136mph on Conrod Straight to Pitt's 144 – but period reports underlined that Pitt 'was decisively outbraked and outdriven by McKay'. Bill Patterson's Cooper-Climax was second, also well ahead of Pitt.

In the six-lap Sedan and Sports Car handicap at the end of the day, Pitt set fastest time against only moderate opposition, McKay and Patterson not taking part.

Bill Pitt in tie and corduroy jacket, relaxing in the seat of XKD 526 – presumably prior to the day's racing.
Terry McGrath Motoring Archives

The Anderson/Pitt era, 1956-1959

'A botched compulsory pit stop by Pitt allowed McKay back into the lead, however, and he went on to win'

Lowood, 3 November 1957
Back in Queensland, at Lowood's Tourist Trophy meeting, Pitt ran in the 30-minute feature event, the Courier-Mail TT.

This time, he and David McKay (Aston Martin DB3S) had a tense battle, with McKay spinning on the first and second laps and allowing Pitt initially to get well ahead. A botched compulsory pit stop by Pitt allowed McKay back into the lead, however, and he went on to win.

McKay did not take part in the four-lap championship scratch race and Pitt prevailed ahead of Arnold Glass's Super Squalo Ferrari, which pressed hard and recorded fastest lap of the day.

In the five-lap Sports and Racing car event, Pitt recorded fastest lap but was unable to overcome a punitive handicap and finished out of the placings.

Gnoo Blas, 27 January 1958
Early in '58 the South Pacific Road Racing Championships came to Gnoo Blas, a circuit formed of public roads close to Orange, New South Wales.

Pitt again chose to compete beyond the D-type's natural realm and started in the South Pacific Championship for Racing Cars, the 100-mile main event. He encountered a problem when his nearside rear wheel started locking under braking, but resumed after a brief stop – now relying more on his gearbox and less on his brakes to slow the car. But a relaxed, polished Brabham (Cooper-Climax) would not be denied and took a clear victory, lapping all but one car in the field and holding plenty in reserve – despite the fact he was not in the race's fastest car. Pitt was fourth and well behind.

The final event was a five-lap handicap race for racing cars, in which Pitt finished sixth while Brabham claimed victory and took a new lap record, at an average speed of just over 100mph.

Lowood, 23 March 1958
Headline event at this meeting was for the Queensland Saloon Car Championships, but Pitt appeared in a four-lap scratch race for cars over 1,500cc and won comfortably enough that he was able to ease up before the end. He also won the A-grade scratch race.

Bathurst, 7 April 1958
The next big outing was the Easter fixture at Bathurst. It was described as a 'fast, spectacular programme' with 20,000 spectators in attendance.

Pitt as usual chose to run with the racing cars rather than the sports cars. In the preliminary three-lap scratch event for racing cars, an exciting tussle in which Pitt finished fifth, the first three places were taken by the Super Squalo Ferrari, a Maserati 300S and a Cooper-Climax.

At Lowood in November 1957, Eric Wendt's XK 120 661097 might have been quick for a car of its type – but the outcome was predictable.
Terry McGrath Motoring Archives

The Bathurst pits, such as they were. Terry McGrath Motoring Archives

The Anderson/Pitt era, 1956-1959

XKD 526 advertised for sale by Westco Motors Pty Limited in Australian Motor Sports, *June 1958.*

Car for sale, June 1958

In the June edition of *AMS*, XKD526 was advertised for sale: 'Mrs Geordie Anderson's successful D-type Jaguar offered for sale. Complete with all factory modifications, enclosed trailer, spares and factory tools. Perhaps the most reliable and successful sports/racing car in the country, it is in first-class condition for the season's racing. It has lapped Lowood in 2m 00s, Bathurst in 2m 57s, Albert Park in 2m 00s and Orange in 2m 21s. Genuine enquiries: W Pitt, Westco Motors Pty Ltd, 49 Mary Street, Brisbane. FA2291.'

A similar advertisement appeared in July 1958 – with some improved lap times substituted.

Offering the car for sale was a sign that Pitt and the Andersons considered that the ability of the car to be really competitive was fast coming to an end – with more ex-works cars coming into Australia, and the appearance of the new generation of sports racers, particularly from Cooper and Lotus. Pitt, however, was destined to continue to race the D-type for another season.

During the course of 1958, the front of the car would be modified slightly, with brake cooling vents inserted into the front of the bonnet on either side of the air intake.

Lowood, 15 June 1958

Pitt was back at Lowood in June for the Queensland Road Racing Championship meeting.

In a scratch race of four laps, won by Stan Jones (Maserati 250F), Pitt finished outside the placings. The main event ran over 20 laps, Stillwell's Maserati not starting (clutch trouble) and Jones's Maserati failing to finish (final drive), but Pitt finished fourth as Alec Mildren (Cooper-Climax) emerged victorious.

Lowood, 31 August 1958

The D-type faced a similar schedule in its next Lowood outing. Pitt was again fourth in the four-lap race, this time behind Ted Gray's Corvette-engined Tornado, Mildren (Cooper-Climax) and Jones (Maserati).

After several retirements (including that of Gray), the 20-lap Lowood Trophy yielded another victory for Alec Mildren with Pitt once again fourth.

Pitt also ran in the Sports and Saloon Car Handicap, where he steadily worked his way through the field mostly of Austin Healeys and MGs, with a couple of Porsches, a Simca and some Holdens thrown in. His was the fastest car in the race, but his heavy handicap kept him out of contention.

Bathurst, 5-6 October 1958

Bathurst hosted the Australian Grand Prix meeting in 1958 – the last occasion on which it did so. Its October fixture would in future become famous in Australia for the nation's biggest touring car meeting.

Lex Davison (Ferrari) won the circuit's final Australian GP, his third victory in the event.

In the Australian Tourist Trophy on the Sunday, 26 laps and 100 miles, Pitt started from the front of the grid and led early, recording 147mph down Conrod Straight. At the end of the second lap, however, he was about 50 yards ahead of Whiteford when he failed to take Murray's Corner, a left-hander at the end of the main straight. He scrambled back onto the track in fifth place, but later suffered brake failure when an oil line severed and sprayed the rear discs.

Pitt fared better in Monday's 10-lap sports car race, coming a close second to Derek Jolly's Lotus. The Matich C-type was third, nearly two minutes astern, with Jack Murray's D-type fourth.

Lowood, 26 October 1958
The Queensland Tourist Trophy meeting did not attract strong fields and in a preliminary event, the Champions Scratch Race over four laps, Pitt was victorious. In the main event, he ran out an easy winner, lapping all but two other competitors.

Albert Park, 23 & 30 November 1958
The Melbourne Grand Prix and Victorian Tourist Trophy events were run over two weekends – the first events at the venue for more than 18 months… and the last for many, many years (it reopened in March 1996, as host of Australia's round of the Formula 1 world championship). Stirling Moss and Jack Brabham appeared, as the international attractions.

On the first Sunday, by-passing the sports car events as usual, Bill Pitt ran in the 25-mile racing car scratch event – a Brabham benefit. Despite starting from the rear of the grid (he had not practised), Brabham's F1 Cooper T45 won by a large margin from Patterson in a similar car. Pitt was seventh.

In the day's main event, the Victorian Tourist Trophy of 100 miles, Pitt took off in the lead and held that position for the first 12 laps, until Whiteford (Maserati 300S) took over. Nearer the end of the race, Pitt was forced wide and hit straw bales at the side of the track at Jaguar Corner, losing about 40s with a pit stop to have the bodywork pulled back from the rear wheel. This cost him second place as he let Ron Phillips's Cooper-Jaguar through.

A sports car scratch race of 25 miles was held before the GP final, Pitt finishing third behind the Whiteford Maserati 300S and Derek Jolly's Lotus XV.

Pitt also started in the Melbourne GP, at the back of the grid, lapping steadily and finishing sixth. Moss prevailed, despite nursing his Cooper T45 with a loss of water, and only Brabham was on the same lap at the end.

> 'On only one occasion was Pitt forced out of a race due to mechanical problems – a tribute to the quality of the product'

Bathurst, 28 March 1959
The Bathurst 100 took place over the Easter weekend, but Pitt swiped a trackside post during practice – and did so hard enough to preclude further participation.

Lowood, 14 June 1959
This would be the final outing for XKD 526 in Bill Pitt's hands – and it was the biggest meeting the Queensland circuit had yet hosted, with the Australian Tourist Trophy as the headline race.

In the main event, the field included Pitt, Frank Matich (C-type XKC 037) and David Finch (XKD 520). While in the lead, Pitt came in to the pits to change a tyre – which turned out to be unnecessary. Ron Phillips (Cooper-Jaguar) roared past to take a lead that he held to the finish, while Pitt took second.

Pitt went again in the Lowood Trophy, with the much quicker racing cars, but was forced out when a stone fractured his goggles.

That marked the end of Pitt's association with XKD 526. As the aforementioned results indicate, on only one occasion was Pitt forced out of a race due to mechanical problems – a tribute to the quality of the product, skilled preparation by Pitt and the Anderson/Westco team and the driver's ability to race the car with appropriate sensitivity.

Pitt and the Andersons looked very seriously at getting a Lister Jaguar, but 'Lofty' England suggested a 3.4 saloon. Pitt thereafter raced the 3.4 with great success: he was second to David McKay in the 1960 Australian Touring Car Championship, won the title in 1961 and was second again in 1962, this time to Bob Jane.

A rear view of the grid at Albert Park in November 1958. Almost 40 years later, the circuit began hosting Australia's round of the F1 World Championship.
Terry McGrath Motoring Archives

The Anderson/Pitt era, 1956-1959

Chapter Three
Frank Matich & Leaton Motors
1959-1961

Frank Matich (1935-2015) hailed from Sydney. In 1958, as a 23-year-old who was mad about motor racing, he took a sales job with Leaton Motors. They ran a business selling used sports cars in suburban Sydney, with retail premises at 299 Princes Highway, Banksia and servicing at 351 Stoney Creek Road, Kingsgrove.

Frank persuaded the owners of the business to accompany him to a motor racing event at Orange, west of Sydney. They were impressed – and that led to the formation of the Leaton Motors racing team.

It wasn't long before Leatons acquired a Jaguar C-type, XKC 037. Being offered the chance to drive it was a highly significant step forward for Matich – and he took another one in July 1959, when Leatons purchased XKD 526 from the Andersons and Pitt. They repainted it in the team's adopted colours of pale yellow with a black stripe down the centre. Between 1959 and 1962 it was thereafter driven, more or less successively, by Matich, Doug Chivas and Barry Topen.

Matich would go on to become one of his country's most distinguished competitors, successfully racing his own eponymous sports cars and single-seaters through the 1960s and remaining competitive until his retirement from the sport in 1974. His accolades include four Australian Tourist Trophy wins, two Australian GP victories and annexing of the Australian Drivers' Championship in 1972.

Frank Matich, right, and Bill Pitt, perhaps with the proprietors of Leaton Motors, discussing the purchase of XKD 526 at the Lowood race circuit in 1959.
Terry McGrath Motoring Archives

Frank Matich & Leaton Motors, 1959-1961

Lowood, 30 August 1959
The D-type made its first appearance as part of the Leaton team at Lowood, in the Queensland Centenary Road Racing Championships.

Matich drove it in the title event – where, as a sign of the times, there were no fewer than six Cooper-Climaxes entered. Matich finished fourth, although some way back from the podium finishers. Alec Mildren won, at the head of a trio of Coopers.

Matich also entered the four-lap B-grade scratch race, in which he set a new sports car lap record at 1m 58s. Having taken the lead at the end of the straight, however, he spun off and had to be satisfied with second in a mixed field of eight cars.

Bathurst, 4 October 1959
The New South Wales Road Racing Championship meeting proved to be a very wet affair.

Matich was there in the D-type and ran in the Sports Cars event. He worked his way up from 13th at the start (after problems in practice) to be third by the seventh lap – having passed Jack Murray in XKD 532. Although he had been carving his way through the field, Matich subsequently had to retire the D-type due to an oil pressure problem.

By November 1959, there were rumours that the Leatons and Matich were due to acquire a Lotus 15, with Doug Chivas scheduled to take over the D-type.

XKD 526 on New South Wales trade plates, receiving some attention in Sydney in 1960.
John Ellacott

Frank Matich & Leaton Motors, 1959-1961

The Australian Tourist Trophy event at Longford, Tasmania, in March 1960. XKD 526 (#87) was driven by Frank Matich and David Finch. Just visible is XKD 520 (#92).
Terry McGrath Motoring Archives

Longford, 5-7 March 1960

The D-type made the trip south to compete in the country's top sports car event, the Australian Tourist Trophy, which attracted a crowd of some 18,000 spectators. By now Jack Brabham was world champion, a success he was to repeat during the season ahead and again in 1966. He competed at this meeting and won all three of his races.

In the TT, Matich in the D-type somehow ended up at the front of the grid, with David Finch in XKD 520 also in the field. But Derek Jolly (driving the Lotus 15 he had shared with Graham Hill at Le Mans in 1959) won the race comfortably. Matich was some way back in third place, while Finch took sixth.

This was to be Frank Matich's last race in the D-type until it was converted in 1961 to comply with the new Gran Turismo class regulations.

Bathurst, 17-18 April 1960

Doug Chivas entered two events in the Leaton D-type at the annual Easter meeting, but did not start either (he had been clocked at more than 140mph for the flying quarter during practice). The car's cubic capacity was by now quoted as 3,770cc, while XKD 520 was listed at 3,800cc – both indicating substantial overbores. The previous October, XKD 526's quoted capacity had been the standard 3,442cc.

Lowood, 12 June 1960

Lowood hosted the Australian Grand Prix meeting and Alec Mildren won the dramatic feature race in his self-built Cooper-Maserati, narrowly beating Lex Davison (Aston Martin DBR4/300). In the 10-lap sports car scratch race, Doug Chivas made his first competitive start at the helm of the Leaton Motors D-type. He battled hard with

The start of the 1960 Tourist Trophy at Longford. The Cooper-Jaguar CJ/1/55 of Ron Phillips seems to have the jump on the D-types of Matich (XKD 526, #87) and Finch (XKD 520, #92). Terry McGrath Motoring Archives

Frank Matich & Leaton Motors, 1959-1961

Doug Chivas in XKD 526 leading Matich's Lotus 15 at Lowood in June 1960. Terry McGrath Motoring Archives

Bob Jane's Maserati 300S and emerged triumphant, with Tom Sulman (Aston Martin) taking third.

Bathurst, 2 October 1960
At the NSW Road Racing Championship meeting, Matich (now in a Lotus 15) was essentially unchallenged en route to winning the 13-lap NSW Sports Car Championship, with Chivas second after Whiteford had spun his Maserati and retired – a one-two for the Leaton Motors team. The three D-types delivered new to Australia all took part in this event, with Jack Murray finishing fifth in XKD 532 while David Finch (XKD 520) did not finish due to a broken oil line. John Ampt was third in his Jaguar-engined Cooper.

The D-type did not run in the Australian Gran Turismo Championship, which was won by Leo Geoghegan's Lotus Elite (his fastest lap time some 15s slower

'The three D-types delivered new to Australia all took part in this event with Jack Murray finishing fifth in XKD 532'

Frank Matich & Leaton Motors, 1959–1961

Bathurst, October 1960: for only the second time, all three Australian D-types competed in the same event. At the wheel of the Leaton Motors XKD 526 (#86), Doug Chivas has stolen a march on the other Leaton-entered car, Matich's Lotus 15. Jack Murray is behind in the silver XKD 532 and, to the right, David Finch is in the ex-Frank Gardner XKD 520. Terry McGrath Motoring Archives

than Chivas had recorded earlier). The race was scarred by tragedy, Reg Smith succumbing to injuries sustained when his Porsche crashed on the Conrod Straight.

In the main event, the Craven A 100-Mile International, Jack Brabham – by now a double world champion, and honoured by a civic reception on the eve of the race – did not disappoint. He took his Cooper T51-Climax to victory as the marque completed a clean sweep of the top five positions.

Gnoo Blas, 3 October 1960
From Bathurst, some teams made the 50-kilometre trip for a Monday fixture at Gnoo Blas, which hosted a programme of four 10-lap races. The sports car event resulted in another Leaton Motors one-two, with Matich's Lotus once again ahead of the D-type.

Warwick Farm, 18 December 1960
There was a significant development in Australian motorsport shortly before Christmas 1960, with the opening of the new Warwick Farm circuit on the outskirts of Sydney (it would remain active until 1973). Torrential rain greeted all involved, including some 21,000 spectators who suffered in the appalling conditions.

In the sports car race, Matich again prevailed in the Lotus with Chivas third behind David McKay's 1,100cc Lola Climax – but Chivas was more than 60s behind Matich in a race that lasted just over 20 minutes.

Doug Chivas rounding Wind Sock corner at the end of Mental Straight (named after the adjacent psychiatric hospital), which led onto the Courseway [sic] at the Gnoo Blas motor racing circuit, Orange. Behind is an Australian-built special, a Buchanan fibreglass body on an MG chassis. Terry McGrath Motoring Archives

Warwick Farm, 29 January 1961

In the new year, the opportunity to see Stirling Moss and a host of other international drivers brought some 65,000 spectators to Warwick Farm – despite searing temperatures (106 degF in the shade). As well as Moss, there were Dan Gurney, Graham Hill, Innes Ireland and Ron Flockhart – plus local hero Jack Brabham.

But conditions were so extreme that only four of the 14 starters finished the main event, the 100-mile International Road Race, amid some bizarre reported maladies such as boiling oil and even boiling fuel. Moss won.

Matich won the five-lap support race for sports cars in his Lotus 15, with Derek Jolly's Lotus second and Chivas in the D-type third.

Catalina Park, 12 February 1961

Sydneysiders were treated to the opening of another new motor racing circuit early in 1961: Catalina Park at Katoomba, in the Blue Mountains just west of the city. This was a short, tight track and thus unlikely to suit the D-type. The inaugural meeting featured 19 short events and attracted a crowd of 15,000. The

Doug Chivas in XKD 526 on the opening day of the Catalina Park circuit, just outside Sydney.
John Ellacott

sports cars competed in a series of heats prior to the final, which yielded yet another win for the Matich Lotus 15 while Chivas placed third.

Warwick Farm, 19 March 1961
Leaton Motors continued its sequence of one-three results, Matich and Chivas on this occasion separated by Murray Carter's 4,660cc Corvette Special in a sports car contest that formed part of an eight-event programme.

Warwick Farm, 21 May 1961
Teams headed back to Warwick Farm in May, when perfect weather helped draw a crowd of 20,000. Bob Jane appeared in his Maserati 300S – but this time with a nicely crafted hardtop to enable the car to qualify for the GT event, a sign of things to come. Matich's Lotus 15 was expected to dominate the sports car event, but it retired after suffering suspension failure when leading on the final lap. It was then up to Chivas in the D-type to rescue the event for the Leaton team, but he spun off at Paddock Bend and John Martin's little Lotus slipped through to win from Chivas. David Finch took fourth in XKD 520.

The aerodynamic enclosed trailer, still on Queensland registration, that was part of the potential sale of XKD 526. Terry McGrath Motoring Archives

Leaton Motors thought about moving on from the D-type before the introduction of the GT class, as evidenced by this advertisement. It is interesting to note that the car was offered with spare engine, spare wheels, three diff ratios and other items, including the trailer. Sports Car World, June 1961

Frank Matich

In the words of respected writer Max Stahl, Frank Matich (1935-2015) 'was considered by many to be Australia's finest all-round race driver'. Frank grew up in Sydney's inner west and, at the age of 15, began an apprenticeship as a diesel engineer at a local oil refinery before moving into the motor trade. He was noted for having 'the gift of the gab', which suited his sales roles during those early days. He became a very successful driver, preferring to race sports cars to single-seaters, but in fact claimed to be more interested in race car design and building.

By 1960 he was competing with distinction in a 2.5-litre Lotus XV provided by Leaton Motors and six years later he built his first car, the Matich SR3 sports-prototype. Matich went on to build other sports and Formula 5000 racers, his meticulous preparation was legendary and he won numerous titles. He resisted all efforts to get him to pursue his career overseas, although he did later do some racing in the USA and New Zealand. Later, he pursued business interests in motorsport and held franchises for Firestone and then Goodyear racing tyres, as well as Bell helmets. Such was the respect in which he was held that he became the only member of the Grand Prix Drivers' Association never to have driven in a Formula 1 race – or even in Europe.

Frank Matich in C-type Jaguar XKC 037 outside Leaton Motors' premises in suburban Sydney. John Ellacott

GT controversy – the D-type hard-top

The new Gran Turismo class had been publicised since early 1960 but seemed really to have gained impetus the following season. David McKay wrote in *Modern Motor* (July 1961): 'Because Australian GT regulations depart from FIA standards by allowing "one-off" specials which could never be used as Grand Touring cars on the open road... there was a great outburst of camouflaging activity. It was obvious that bona fide GT cars wouldn't stand a chance against fire-breathing sports-racers that had already been "converted" – so even those of us who had held out until now got busy cooking up GT rockets. Leaton Motors top-dressed its D-type Jag with a shapely roof that looked fine from a distance but fairly rough close at hand...'

The D-type's aluminium top was built by Alan Standfield – the 'go to' aluminium body man in Sydney at the time. In 1957-58 Standfield had built a 'long nose' bonnet for XKD 520 and this was not the last time he would see XKD 526. He used a Perspex windscreen and a series of small bolts to attach the top.

It has to be said that the D-type's new look was quite attractive – particularly in circumstances where speed of manufacture would have been a greater priority than styling – but some of the other conversions seemed to be competing strongly for the ugliness prize, not least Carter's Corvette Special and the Lola 1100.

Frank Matich & Leaton Motors, 1959-1961

The newly installed hardtop actually suited the car very well and was expertly made by top Sydney race car builder Alan Standfield.
Terry McGrath Motoring Archives

Catalina Park, 9 July 1961

The D-type 'GT' made its first appearance at Catalina Park in July, at a meeting that featured a flurry of short events in very cold conditions. Frank Matich drove the Lotus 15 in two races, winning comfortably – but the D-type was also in his hands for the over 1,500cc sports car race (rather than the GT class). He won that comfortably, despite an Austin Healey hitting the Jaguar's door and sending him into a spin.

Warwick Farm, 30 July 1961

There was another big crowd at Warwick Farm for the Australian GT Championship meeting. Most competing cars in that event were, like the D-type, converted sports-racers. In the final, run over 50 miles, Matich disappeared over the horizon and the Jaguar eventually lapped almost the whole field, David McKay (Lola 1100 coupé) being the only other driver on the same lap at the end.

Catalina Park, 27 August 1961

The idea of winter motor racing in Katoomba seems counter-intuitive to anyone familiar with the area… and rain and fog duly prevailed. Frank Matich drove the D-type to wins in both GT races, the first of four laps and the second of six. He beat a couple of Buckles, Sydney-built fibreglass coupés with Ford Zephyr power.

Bathurst, 1 October 1961

The October long weekend event at Bathurst was more subdued than usual, with modest entries, many non-appearances and a crowd of only about 10,000.

Sunday's main feature was the Australian Tourist Trophy of 75 miles (19 laps). Bib Stillwell had just imported a Cooper-Monaco and practice showed that he was clearly the man to beat. Frank Matich had crashed the Lotus 15 the week before during private practice and damaged his wrist, so had to run in the D-type – no match for Stillwell's Cooper. There was some very close racing between Matich and the five-litre Corvette Special of Murray Carter, resulting in Carter easing ahead – but then he retired with brake problems. At the end, the D-type was the only car on the same lap as Stillwell, ahead of Bob Jane's Maserati 300S and a Cooper-Climax.

Frank Matich & Leaton Motors, 1959-1961

November 1961: Bob Jane (later to own and race the Lightweight E-type S850667) also had a hardtop conversion carried out on his Maserati 300S, chassis #3059. XKD 526 can be seen in the background. Terry McGrath Motoring Archives

Matich did win the 13-lap New South Wales Road Racing Championship for GT cars, setting a lap record and again finishing comfortably ahead of Jane's Maserati 300S, which spun three times and had brake problems. This was to be Matich's last race in the D-type, however, his relationship with Leaton Motors coming to an end – with litigation to follow.

**Warwick Farm,
5 November 1961**
Doug Chivas was back in the D-type on its next appearance, in a 10-lap GT race, and took an early lead that he held to the end to defeat Leo Geoghegan's Lotus Elite. That was Doug's last competitive outing in the car. Bib Stillwell won the main event, the 23-lap Sam Hordern Trophy race, in his 2.5-litre Cooper-Climax.

**Warwick Farm,
17 December 1961**
For the balance of its mainstream career, XKD 526 would be in the hands of Barry Topen. Despite being new to the D-type, he finished second in the over 1,500cc sports car scratch race, behind John Martin (now driving the Leaton Lotus 15). On the track both were behind Bib Stillwell (Cooper-Monaco), but he would be disqualified for a push start.

**Catalina Park,
21 January 1962**
There were no fewer than 18 events scheduled at the next Catalina Park meeting. Topen took victories in both a four-lap GT race and an eight-lapper that featured a very mixed field. He set a new class record and also finished third behind two Lotuses in the 12-lap feature race.

**Warwick Farm,
4 February 1962**
A reported 70,000 crowd attended Warwick Farm in February – Stirling Moss and Jack Brabham once more the drawcards. Moss won the main event in a field chiefly composed of Cooper-Climaxes. This time, immediately afterwards, he helicoptered away to catch a plane to Florida…

In the five-lap GT race, Barry Topen took an immediate lead and won comfortably from a Lotus Elite, Bob Jane's Maserati having suffered a transmission failure very soon after the start. Topen set a new GT class record, the D-type's best lap yet at Warwick Farm.

Sandown, 12 March 1962
The new Sandown circuit's opening event was a big one, with many international drivers lured to Melbourne's first motor racing event since Albert Park closed in 1958. They included Moss, Brabham, Bruce McLaren, John Surtees, Roy Salvadori, Ron Flockhart, Chuck Daigh and Jim Clark. Several had left their cars in Australia after earlier events at Warwick Farm and Lakeside.

Jack Brabham (Cooper T55-Climax) won the 120-mile main event, with Moss back in fifth in an ill-handling Lotus 21.

Barry Topen drove the D-type into second place in an initial five-lap GT event, behind Murray Carter's Corvette Special. In the 25-lap Kevin Lott Sports Car Trophy, Topen finished third behind the Leaton Lotus 15 of John Martin and Stillwell's Cooper-Monaco.

In the main GT scratch event over 10 laps, however, the D-type came to grief, skidding on oil and

crashing through a safety barrier into a gully. Topen was not badly hurt, but the accident did herald the end of XKD 526's serious racing career...

The road to recovery

The D-type's bonnet section was not beyond repair; it was crumpled, pushed back and up, and so Leatons asked Alan Standfield to repair it.

By this time their business had substantial financial problems and, in June 1963, they offered the Lotus 15 and the D-type (with bus and trailer) for sale in SCW, with the following description: 'For Sale. The complete Leaton Motors Racing Team. Selling as a team or individually, they comprise: 2½-litre Lotus Climax 15, beaten only once in its career. Second string, another well-known car – the "D" Jag that has been resprayed British Racing Green and still has the hard-top fitted. Racing in GT Formula this car was defeated only once and, in 1961, was the Australian GT champion. It is suitable for road or track work.

'Also for sale. The well-known LEATON bus, D-trailer and spares for both cars. 'For further particulars, contact: Mr GEORGE LEATON. Leaton Motors (Sydney) Pty Ltd, 299 Princes Highway, Banksia, NSW.'

In November 1964 the following advertisement appeared: 'Jaguar D racing coupé, winner of many races on all tracks. Released now – for sale at $1850. Very good condition throughout. Principals contact Ron Dunbier Motors Pty Ltd, 299 Princes Highway, Banksia 59 4303 59 0286.'

The seller was a Sydney suburban car dealer who had taken over the Leaton address and even its telephone number.

In 1965, the car was in the hands of Michael Crampton, a motor mechanic with premises in Kingsway, in the southern Sydney suburb of Gymea. He sold it to Keith Russell.

Following the D-type's accident at Sandown, XKD 526 would appear on the race track again – this time sporting a new colour scheme Terry McGrath Motoring Archives

Interestingly, XKD 526 had been resprayed in its original British Racing Green when offered for sale in 1963, but no photographs have come to light with it in BRG with the hardtop still in place. Sports Car World, June 1963

From the driving seat

In conversation with Graham Howard, Barry Topen retained fond memories of XKD 526: 'I suppose I drove the last winning races for the car. I ran it at Warwick Farm, Katoomba and Sandown, and set new lap records at each of them. The maximum it reached at Sandown was probably 140mph – and even at that speed it was tremendously stable. Well, it was giving you a ride, bouncing about a bit, but I was enjoying it. It was a lovely feeling. I would love to have been on the Mulsanne Straight aiming for 200.

'It was built like an aircraft and it felt like an aircraft – an early light aircraft. The whole car was outstanding, no doubt about it. It was a very exciting car to drive and felt very solid.'

The words "released now" were puzzling – perhaps an indirect reference to Leaton Motors' financial woes? Sydney Morning Herald, 21 November 1964

Chapter Four
Racing winds down
1965-1967

Keith Maurice Russell ran a panel repair shop under the name Able Industries at 404 Canterbury Road in the Sydney suburb of Campsie, doing mostly insurance repair work. He also appears to have organised a small racing team, operating as Able Industries Car Club or similar, and a Turner also ran under the Able name. He repainted the D-type in his trademark blue and white colour scheme, the lower part of the car in white with blue on the upper section 'bleeding' in.

Russell evidently changed – or wanted to change – XKD 526's engine in the car, as the following advertisement placed by him appeared in the *Sydney Morning Herald* on Saturday 16 October 1965: 'Jag D-type eng, as new, any inspect. $150. 78-8351.'

Russell was listed as having entered an event at Hume Weir in December 1965, but might not actually have taken part. His first competitive outing with the car is believed to have been in January 1966, at Catalina Park.

One commentator noted that the car on that occasion 'lacked old form', but Russell was clearly not pushing the car hard and it was entered as having an engine capacity of 3.8 litres. The block observed in the car upon its return to the UK in 2015 was of 3.8 litres and probably dates back to this time.

Russell then appeared in XKD 526 at Warwick Farm on 13 February 1966, contesting the Division 1 sports car race without a notable result.

He also ran at Hume Weir on the NSW/Victoria border over Easter 1966, with a crowd of some 9,000 in attendance. In a four-lap sports car race, Russell was going quite well in second place until he locked the brakes up and skidded into a wall. Three months later he was running at Oran Park near Sydney at the 3 July meeting. Russell was entered in two events for sports and racing cars. In the first of them he managed a third place.

Hume Weir was a circuit down on the NSW/Victoria border, but the other three circuits were in or near Sydney.

'One commentator noted that the car on that occasion 'lacked old form', but Russell was clearly not pushing the car hard'

Racing winds down, 1965-1967

In 1965 Keith Russell advertised the engine for sale. It is understood not to have been sold then, but the original block could not later be located.

At Warwick Farm in 1967, the original D-type wheels were still fitted. Terry McGrath Motoring Archives

Chapter Five

A long love affair
1967-2014

On 21 January 1967 Russell advertised the car for sale in the *Sydney Morning Herald*, being careful not to expend too much money on too descriptive and lengthy an ad: 'D-type. Excellent condition. $1850. 78 8351.'

Keith Berryman, then 26 years of age, saw the advertisement and bought the car for £1,700. This was at a time when a good used XK 150 Fixed Head Coupé could be purchased from a Sydney dealer for about $1,200. Berryman had grown up in a farming family from Stockinbingal, near Cootamundra in western NSW, and had had some local competition experience – but none in circuit racing. He drove the car some 250 miles from Sydney back to his farm.

XKD 526 came with the 3.8-litre block (apparently still with the original head), 15x8in wheels, flared rear guards, the distinctive blue and white Keith Russell paint job, the hardtop still fitted, a proper windscreen and three Weber carburettors. There had been no discussion about the whereabouts of the original block during the purchase. In March 1967 Berryman road-registered the car and obtained a logbook from the Confederation of Australian Motor Sports.

Berryman carried out just routine servicing, as a compression test on the engine was satisfactory and the oil pressure was good. On 13 August 1967 it had its first competitive outing in his hands at Amaroo Park, on the outskirts of Sydney.

Thereafter he modified the road wheels, which were unsafe, and also removed the hardtop, which involved replacing the original windscreen that had come with the car. He also gave the car a repaint in a medium shade of blue.

His next race outing was at Warwick Farm in February 1968.

XKD 526 at the Berryman farm at Stockinbingal, NSW, wide mag wheels and flared wheel arches quite evident. Heinz Schendzielorz

A long love affair, 1967-2014

A long love affair, 1967-2014

'Cummins knew that D-type designer Malcolm Sayer was from an aircraft background and it was clear he would need, among other tradesmen, a riveting expert'

Another shot of XKD 526 at the Stockinbingal farm, shortly before some of the car was taken to Sydney to enable its long restoration (and that of XKD 510) to commence. Ian Cummins Estate

Keith Berryman in XKD 526 at Hume Weir, now minus its canopy. Terry McGrath Motoring Archives

Berryman does not recall the result, but remembers being hit from behind by one of the car's previous drivers, Doug Chivas. The impact dented the spare wheel area and triggered another visit to Alan Standfield's Mascot workshop for repairs.

There were a further two outings at Hume Weir, these being in April and September 1968. This was another tight circuit, but Berryman was happy with the way the car performed. In June 1970 the car also ran at Oran Park.

On Sunday 6 September 1970, Keith averaged 70mph to win the first Tom Sulman Trophy for Historic Sports and Racing Cars, run over 13 laps at Warwick Farm. He finished just over a second ahead of Noel Barnes in a supercharged MG TC Special, with an Aston Martin DB2 and the Dalro Jaguar Special among the diverse field that had been in pursuit.

From about 1971 the car remained stored in a shed at the Berryman farm, its road registration having lapsed in March 1969.

Later to become Australia's best-known Jaguar enthusiast, Ian Cummins acquired the remains of D-type XKD 510 in 1974. He had recently restored C-type XKC 037 and his D-type acquisition was highly significant in the story of the ultimate restoration of XKD 526, as the cars were to occupy the same workshop for some six years.

Cummins knew that D-type designer Malcolm Sayer was from

an aircraft background and it was clear he would need, among other tradesmen, a riveting expert. Qantas provided what he required. He was very fortunate to find Bill Colyer, a perfectionist sheet-metal worker who carried out heavy maintenance on Boeing 747s. At the same time, it became clear that it would be essential to have another D-type from which jigs could be made, to enable XKD 510's rebuild to be possible. This meant the 'pattern' car would also need to be at least partly dismantled.

On the face of it, that would be an enormous challenge in Australia – but, fortunately, Ian knew where to look. He telephoned Keith Berryman, gently persuading him that this was going to be the opportunity to have XKD 526 restored.

In October 1975, he paid a visit to the Berryman farm. Cummins and Berryman partly stripped XKD 526 in the barn and the central section – the monocoque tub – was taken back to Sydney. The remainder of the car, including the instrument panel, the bonnet and rear body section, the front frame, the engine and gearbox and the rear axle/suspension assembly, remained at the farm. Its recorded mileage at the time was 6,741.

Berryman at a later stage delivered the rest of the car to Cummins in Sydney. Work proceeded with several tradesmen at Classic Autocraft, repairing and making up new skins and panels as required. After the bodywork had been shaped and tested for fit, it was ready to go back on the car. Bill Colyer's job was then to rivet it all together in the course of general reassembly.

The following items were noted in relation to the restoration of the bodywork:

the top scuttle panel was replaced; the front section of the nose was replaced, in order to restore the shape of the intake to the original, from its more rectangular profile introduced during past repairs in Brisbane; the air vents in the tops of the rear mudguards were filled in having been cut into the car during or before 1960; the air vents on either side of the bonnet mouth were retained, although these had not been part of the car originally and after some debate, a fin was added,

Bathurst 1986: Keith Berryman at the wheel of XKD 526, giving John Goss a lift around the Mt Panorama track prior to the start of the James Hardie 1000. Goss would start the race in his Citibank Jaguar XJS, having won the event the previous year in a TWR-entered XJS with Armin Hahne as co-driver.
Terry McGrath Motoring Archives

A long love affair, 1967-2014

Keith and Sandra Berryman depart the scene of the March 1989 National Jaguar Rally Concours in Canberra, with Ian and Anne Cummins following in XKD 510.
John Elmgreen

similar to that on the works cars; a new front subframe was constructed with great care taken to preserve the original with the car as this was still showing the car's chassis number stamping.

XKD 510 was finally completed in 1981 and, with that done, attention could be focussed upon the restoration of XKD 526 with the benefit of the lessons learned while doing 510. The work was finished the following year. In June 1983 it appeared at the National Jaguar Rally in Albury, where it won the concours.

After the car had been restored, it was not raced or road-registered again but was used from time to time as a promotional car by Jaguar in Australia. Such events included the Australian Grand Prix, introduced to the F1 world championship calendar for the first time in 1985, other racing events and some new Jaguar model launches. One positive spin-off for Berryman was that this gave him the opportunity to meet some legendary motor

Porter Profiles – Jaguar D-type • XKD 526

A long love affair, 1967-2014

The D-type and Spitfire at Temora airfield in July 2003. Courtesy of Temora Aviation Museum

racing figures, including Stirling Moss and many others. In fact, Moss drove XKD 526 on several different occasions.

There were also a couple of novelty events in which the D-type 'raced' a Spitfire. The first was at quite a big air show in the NSW country town of Wagga on 2 November 1997. The Jaguar and Spitfire lined up side by side and had to travel to the other end of the airstrip, turn around and come back. The D-type was first back to the control tower finishing line by about 50 metres. The second was on 6 July 2003 at Temora in rural NSW, where a highly acclaimed aviation museum is located. There were two runs, one on Saturday and one on Sunday. The Saturday run was won by the D-type, but Berryman felt that winning twice would not be a good thing and he therefore took it easier on the Sunday.

> 'The Jaguar and Spitfire lined up side by side and had to travel to the other end of the airstrip, turn around and come back. The D-type was first back to the control tower...'

Proving the cynics wrong

Following his acquisition of XKD 510, Ian Cummins spent time in England before restoring both that car and, later, XKD 526. He said, 'I started finding out everything I could about D-types. I photographed every one I could, even measuring distances between the rivets, trying to get every detail. When I was showing photos of the wreck around in England, several of the motoring boys there said it was a mammoth job. They felt it would be possible in England because of the expertise they had, but in Australia we wouldn't have the tradesmen or the know-how. I'd seen some of their restorations and was definitely not impressed. That made me all the more determined to get on with it, just to show them.'

The D-type at Wagga airfield, NSW, in November 1997, about neck and neck with the Spitfire.
Geoff Breust

Chapter Six
Back to the UK
2014

After almost 50 years as XKD 526's custodian, Keith finally decided to part with the car. He offered it quietly to a couple of likely local buyers, in the hope that it could stay in Australia, but without success. In due course a buyer came forward from England.

Before the sale was confirmed, renowned D-type expert Chris Keith-Lucas was sent out from England in June 2014 to go over the car and report back. He was in Australia for little more than 24 hours. Neither Chris nor Keith knew the buyer's identity except that he was a US collector. This gentleman ultimately did not go ahead with the purchase for reasons unrelated to the car. However, Chris' visit and report were far from wasted, and it was just a few months before we learned that the car would be purchased by none other than Jo Bamford, the next generation of the heavy plant JCB family. The car was duly shipped out to England, with the original front frame and the 1960s hardtop included.

Following its return to the UK, by July 2015 the car had been further evaluated by CKL and restoration work was carried out. No major bodywork was done, but the car was repainted in the original dark British Racing Green including, for authenticity, the previously polished alloy interior. The seats were also retrimmed in the original production D-type style.

The cylinder head was confirmed as the original and rebuilt, as was the multi-plate Borg & Beck clutch. Some unrepaired suspension damage from past accidents was also found and corrected, and the suspension refinished in black where it had been red. The Girling shock absorbers were found to be original – and still serviceable. The presence of the ZF limited-slip differential was

XKD 526 was re-registered in the UK in 2015 after the restoration work carried out by CKL Developments

Back to the UK, 2014

also observed, a rarity usually only seen in Works and Ecurie Ecosse cars. A number of other servicing matters were likewise attended to, as well as items required to qualify the car for historic racing. The car was allocated a UK registration, 12 RW, and by 2018 had a recorded mileage of 7,578.

The most significant part of CKL's work, however, was the restoration of the original chassis frame. It had been considered too damaged to re-use at the time of the Cummings restoration, and Keith Berryman had stored this since that time. However CKL, having experience in this operation, the necessary D-type chassis jig and sufficient Reynolds 531 tubing, were able to correct the damage and alignment without losing its basic originality. This original frame was then refitted in the car where it now happily resides to the benefit of the car's provenance. That September Jo Bamford was able to fulfil his ambition to race the car at the Goodwood Revival Meeting.

In 2018 the car was sold once again via UK-based classic car dealer Martin Chisholm and a new registration number 353 UYU allocated. At this time, the decision was made to once again employ the skills of Chris Keith-Lucas's company CKL Engineering to return the body back to its original configuration without the fin and to replace the non-standard rivets with those of the correct specification as used by Jaguar. This also provided a valuable insight into the originality of the panel work, and enabled CKL to distinguish the major proportion of panels which had remained untouched from day one from those that had been repaired after its several racing scrapes.

At this time quite serious consideration was given to the possibility of re-fitting the hard top. In the end it was decided not to go ahead, but as this item represents a significant period of the car's history, a wheeled display frame was made so that the hard top can be viewed with the car.

The final word

Almost all D-types have a competition history, even the production models that were neither works cars nor entered in major events around the world. Competition cars are damaged from time to time and then rebuilt by their owners, who regard that process as a simple by-product of their desire to go racing. Works cars are rebuilt at the factory, others with whatever spare parts and general skills or facilities are available at the relevant time and place.

So it was with XKD 526.

It was raced by highly skilled, established drivers in Australia – particularly Bill Pitt and Frank Matich. It suffered three racing mishaps in its early days – in December 1956 at Albert Park, March 1959 at Bathurst and March 1962 at Sandown. It was also crashed again in April 1966, at Hume Weir. No-one was hurt and each time it was rebuilt locally, on the first two occasions in Brisbane, with the benefit of whatever facilities were available to local Jaguar dealers the Andersons at the time, and on subsequent occasions in Sydney, by suburban panel shops. From 1975 to 1983, it was to have yet another rebuild, again in Sydney, under the guidance of Australia's leading classic Jaguar specialist Ian Cummins, who was determined to do the job correctly as he restored his own XKD 510 at the same time.

It has the history of a car that was seriously raced in its heyday – and the aforementioned incidents form part of its pedigree. It has the benefit of a continuous known history and it has no competing contenders as the 'real' XKD 526.

Fortunately its original front frame, stamped with the chassis number, has always remained with the car and is now part of it once again, eliminating any possibility of a recreation based on no more than that component. It lost its original cylinder block many years ago, but that is hardly unexpected. To anyone that has studied XKD 526 closely in recent years, its remarkable number of original parts has been a delightful surprise – particularly after more than 60 years.

Clockwise: the ZF differential found in the car in 2015 in the course of CKL's restoration work. The engine on a stand at CKL in 2015 – the original head and dry sump system with a replacement block. The original front chassis frame on CKL's jig after cleaning up but before its restoration. The outriggers, removed in Australia, were subsequently reinstated. The rivets used in the reassembly of the car in the course of the restoration in Sydney in the late 1970s/early 1980s – here shown in 2015 at CKL. These had larger heads than the originals.

Back to the UK, 2014

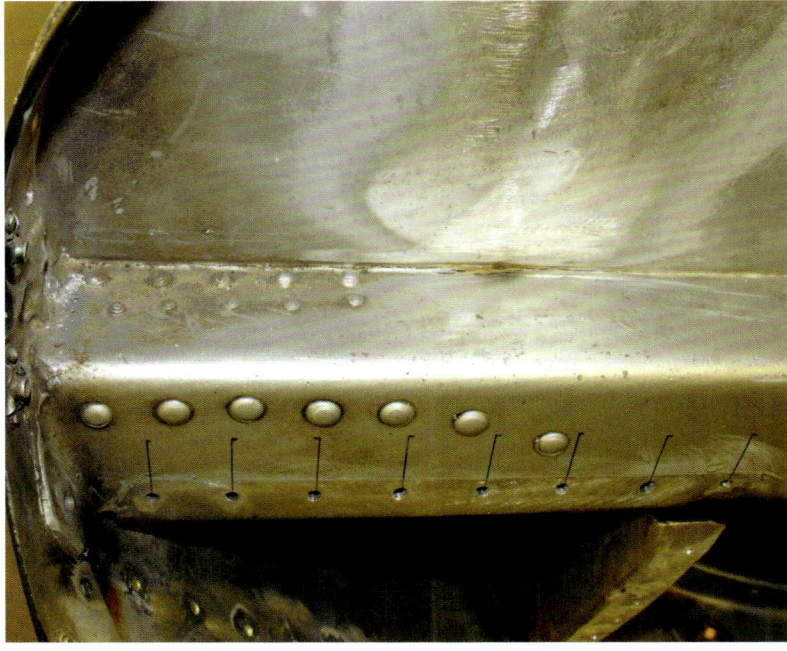

Chapter Seven
XKD 526 in detail
Studio photography by John Colley
Text by Philip Porter

Often known as 'an aircraft on wheels', the D-type was a masterpiece of automotive sculpture. Designer Malcolm Sayer hated to be called a stylist, however, and was, above all, an aerodynamicist. An extraordinary man, he worked with a long-hand form of what today we call Computer Aided Design to produce a series of figures from which the craftsmen in the Prototype Shop at Jaguar would build the formers on which the bodies would be created.

The aircraft analogy is a good one as a number of features were borrowed from the aviation world, such as rubber bag tanks for the fuel. Indeed, Engineering Director Bill Heynes referred in his notes from the start to the D-type's 'fuselage'. The Jaguar factory had spent much of the war building sections of aircraft and so valuable lessons were learnt and would later be applied to the competition cars.

Other innovations featured on the D-types were alloy wheels, semi-monocoque construction, dry-sump engine lubrication and, of course, the disc brakes first seen on the 1953 C-types.

As I have written before, in creating the D-type, Sayer brought science to the art of racing car design, and scientifically created a work of art.

The D-type publicly introduced Malcolm Sayer's elliptical mouth design that would become such an iconic feature of Jaguar's sports cars for many decades to come. Can anyone deny that the D-type is pure sculptural beauty?

XKD 526 in detail

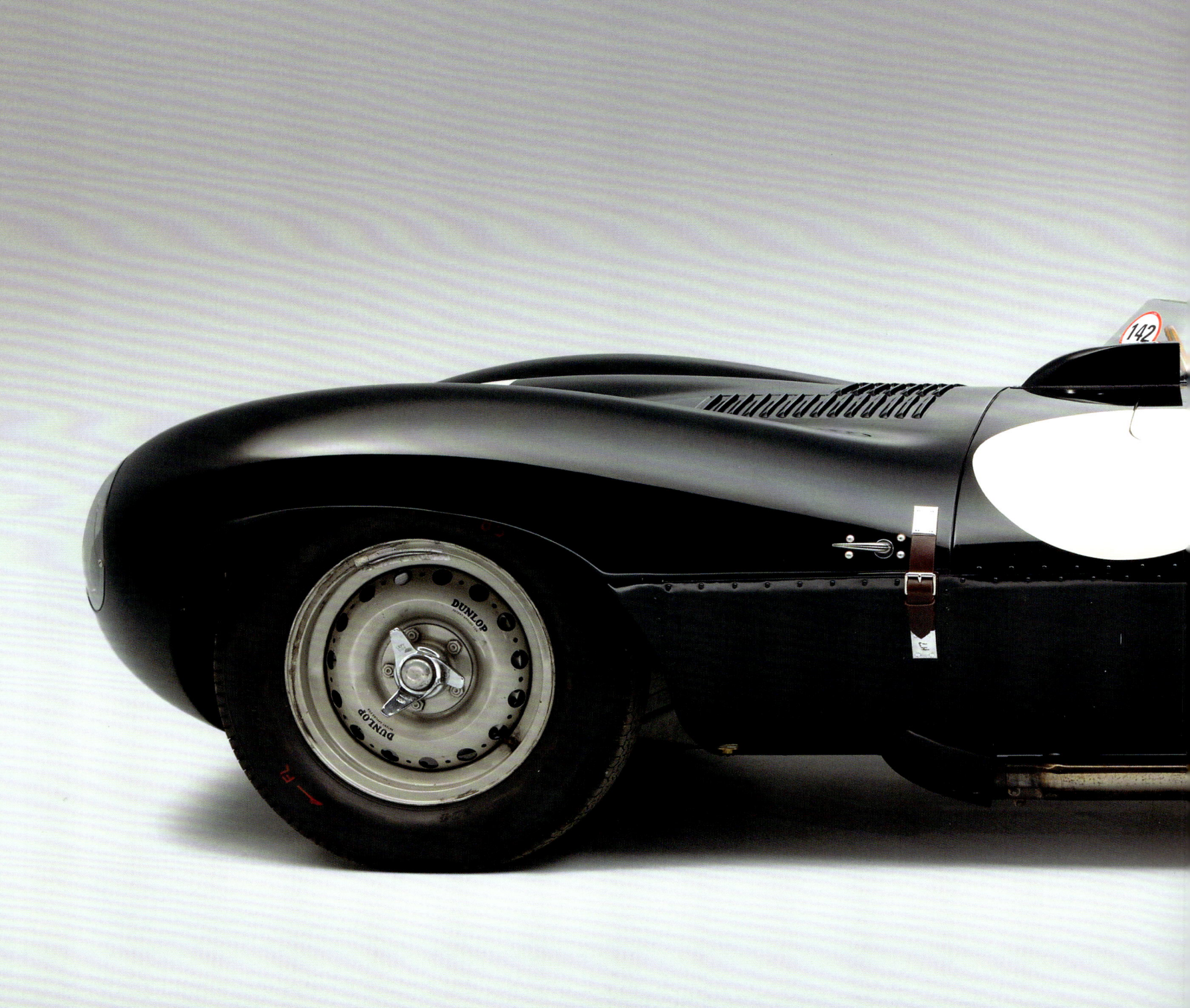

XKD 526 in detail

The brilliant XK engine, first introduced in 1948, showed a remarkable facility for development. The adoption of Weber carburettors boosted power. Dry-sumping the engine helped to decrease the frontal area in comparison with the C-type, and the oil tank was positioned outboard of the exhaust manifolds.

XKD 526 in detail

XKD 526 in detail

Whereas you climb into a C-type, you 'put on' a D-type. The driving position feels far more enclosed and embracing. The four-speed 'box was easily accessed from above and, when not in use, the passenger area was covered by a removable rigid tonneau cover.

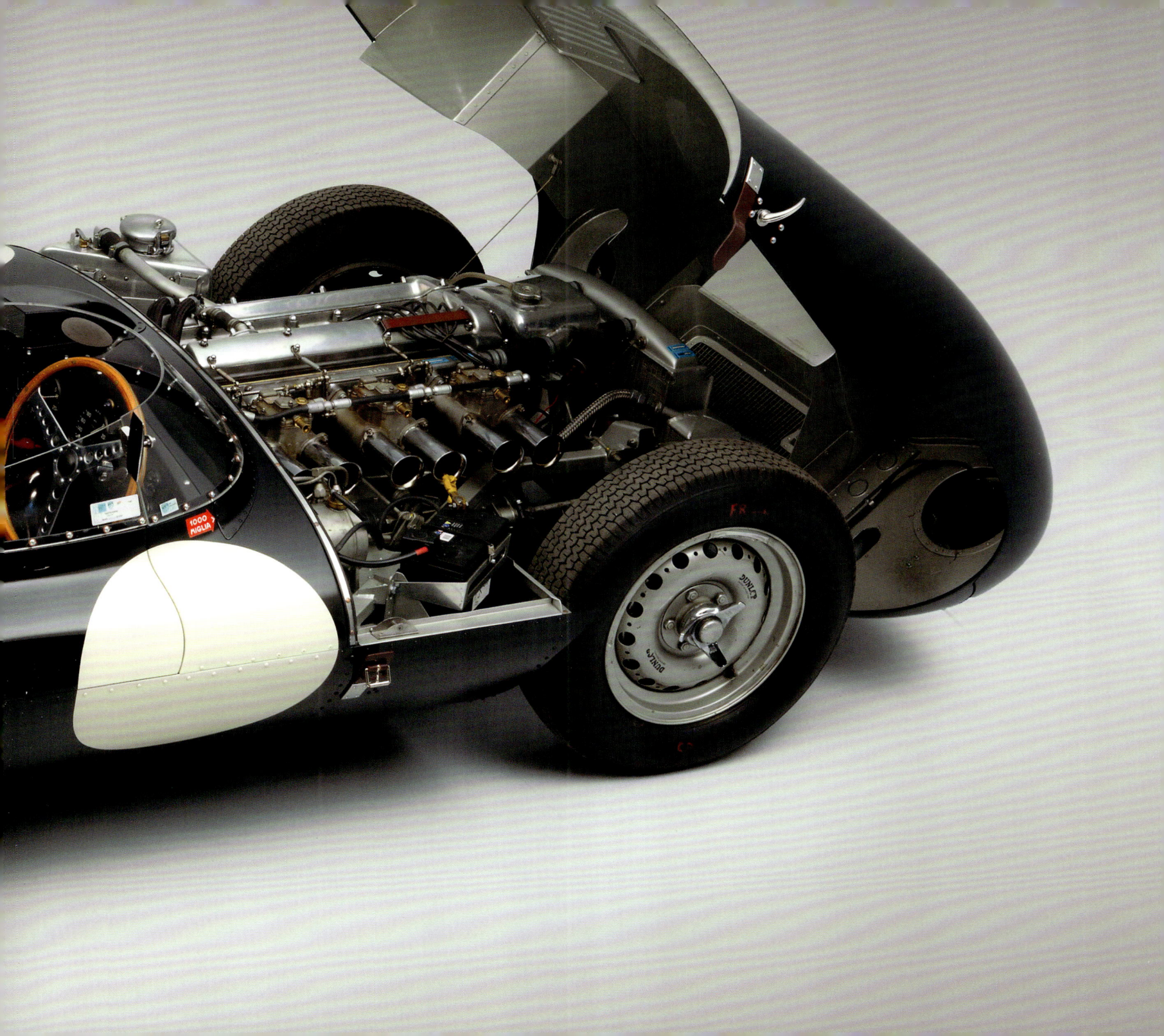

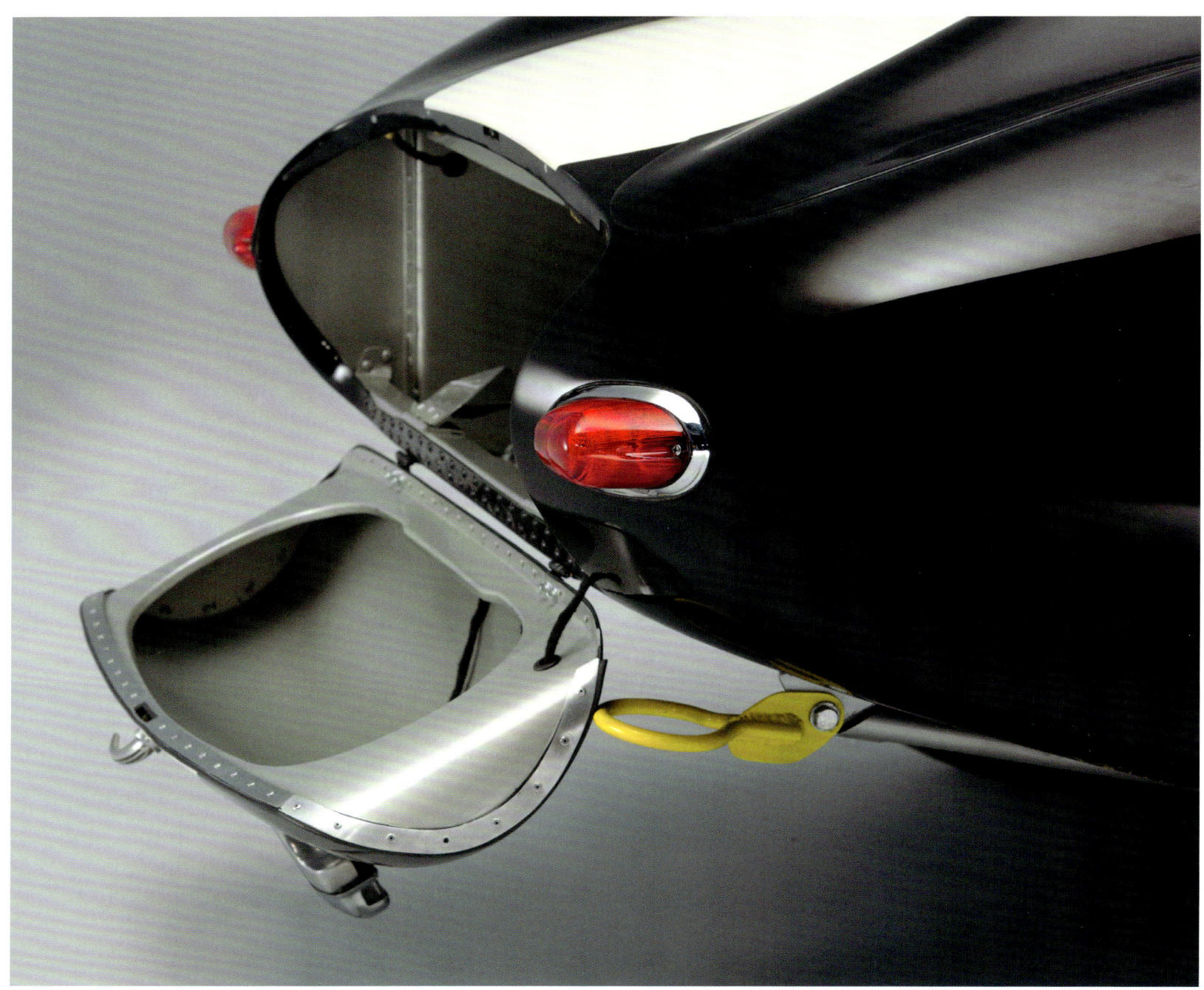

XKD 526 in detail

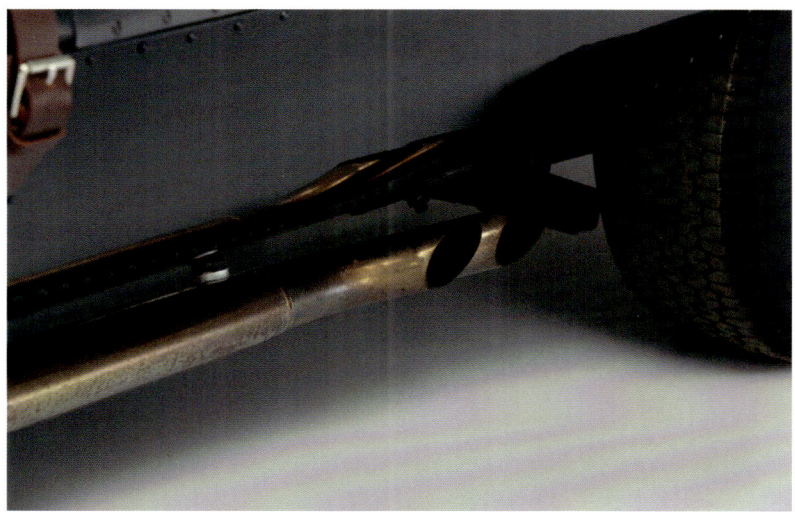

The spare wheel lived in the tail, an area that makes a useful boot (trunk) if one goes without a spare. Having side exhausts kept ride height to a minimum and contributed to minimising drag. Aircraft practice was extensively employed in the construction of the shell with visible rivets.

XKD 526 in detail

XKD 526's long and illustrious Australian motor racing career is well illustrated by the wide variety of events for which programmes are retained with the car. Sayer was obsessive about keeping his designs 'clean' with as little as possible to interrupt airflow. The original aluminium hard-top, built by Alan Standfield in the early 1960s is still with the vehicle.

XKD 526 in detail

XKD 526 in detail

Although we all refer to Jaguar's three-time Le Mans winner as the D-type, in factory paperwork they were always known as the XK 120D, or even occasionally as the XK 140D. Whatever the name used, the trusty XK engine and Sayer's wind-cheating design meant the D was capable of prodigious maximum speeds, even by today's standards.

Index

Abbott, James 30
Abercrombie, Jimmy 13, 15
Able Industries 54
Albert Park 11, 22, 23, 25, 26-28, 30, 35, 36, 51, 66
   Argus Trophy 23
   Australian Tourist Trophy 22
   Sports Car Scratch 28, 36
   Victorian Tourist Trophy 26-28, 36
   Victorian Trophy Handicap 28
Ampt, John 43
Anderson family 10, 12, 13, 15, 25, 35, 16-37, 38, 66
Anderson, Cyril 12, 13, 15
Anderson, Doris 'Geordie' 11, 12-13, 15, 16, 35
Anderson/Westco Team 36
Andersons Agencies 12
Amaroo Park 56
Around Australia Trial 13
   Ladies Trophy 13
Aston Martin 43
   DB2 59
   DB3S 26, 33
   DB3S (DB3S9) 31
   DBR4/300 42
Attwood, Richard 11
Ausca 30
Austin Healey 35, 49
   100S 16
Australian Drivers' Championship 38
Australian Gran Turismo Championship 43

Australian Motor Sports 23, 35
Australian Touring Car Championship 36
Australian Tourist Trophy 38
Bamford, Jo 64, 66
Barnes, Noel 59
Barrett, Alf 15
Bathurst 18, 21, 25, 31, 33, 35, 36, 40, 42, 43, 45, 49-51, 66
   100 36
   Australian Tourist Trophy 35, 49
   Craven A 100 Mile International 45
   New South Wales (NSW) Championship for Racing Cars 31
   New South Wales (NSW) Championship for Sports Cars 31
   New South Wales (NSW) Road Racing Championship 19, 40, 43, 51
   Sedan and Sports Car handicap 31
Behra, Jean 22, 23, 25, 28
Bell (helmets) 48
Berryman, Keith 13, 25, 56, 59, 60, 61, 63, 66
Borg & Beck (clutch) 64
Bottrill, Les 10, 66
Brabham, Jack 25, 28, 30, 33, 36, 42, 45, 46, 51
Brisbane Motor Show 15
Carter, Murray 47, 48, 49, 51
Catalina Park 46-47, 49, 51, 54
Chisholm, Martin 66
Chivas, Doug 38, 40, 42, 43, 45, 46, 47, 51, 59

CKL Engineering 66
Clark, Jim 51
Classic Autocraft 60
Colyer, Bill 60
Confederation of Australian Motorsports 56
Cooper 28, 35, 40, 49
   Cooper-Climax 25, 31, 33, 35, 40, 51
   Cooper-Holden 30
   Cooper-Jaguar 36, 42, 43
   Cooper-Maserati 42
   Cooper-Monaco 49, 51
   Cooper T45 36
   Cooper T51-Climax 36, 45
   Cooper T55-Climax 51
Corvette Special 47, 48, 49, 51
Crampton, Michael 53
Cummins, Anne 61
Cummins, Ian 13, 59, 60, 63, 66
Daigh, Chuck 51
Dalro-Jaguar Special 59
Davey, Jack 11
Davison, Lex 28, 30, 31, 35, 42
Dunbier, Ron 53
England, 'Lofty' 26, 36
Ferrari 35
   500/625 28
   Super Squalo 22, 30, 33
FIA 48
Finch, David 11, 36, 41, 42, 43, 45, 47
Firestone 48
Flockhart, Ron 46, 51
Ford

Customline 25
   Zephyr 49
Formula 1 22, 48
   (F1) World Championship 36, 61
Formula 5000 48
Gardner, Frank 11, 30, 45
Gaze, Tony 13, 15
Geoghegan, Leo 43, 51
Girling (shock absorbers) 64
Glass, Arnold 33
Gnoo Blas 33, 45
   South Pacific Road Racing Championships 33
Goodwood Revival 66
Goodyear (tyres) 48
Goss, John 60
Gran Turismo Class (GT Class) 42, 48
Grand Prix
   Australian 13, 22, 23, 25, 35, 42, 61
   Drivers' Association 48
   Melbourne 36
Green, Barry 18, 22
Gray, Ted 35
Griffiths, Arthur 16
Gurney, Dan 46
HWM Jaguar 16
Hahne, Armin 60
Hawkes, Tom 30
Heynes, Bill 68
Hill, Graham 42, 46
Holden 35
Howard, Graham 53
Hughes, Les 13

Hume Weir 54, 59, 66
Ireland, Innes 46
Jaguar (cars) 8, 11, 13, 18, 19, 36, 59, 63
    C-type 8, 13, 15, 30, 35, 36, 38, 48, 59, 73, 77
    D-type 8-15, 16, 25, 28, 30, 31, 35, 40, 42, 43, 45, 46, 47, 48, 49, 51, 53, 54, 56, 59, 60, 63, 64, 66
    D-type 'GT' 49
    E-type 11, 51
    Mk I 13, 15
    Mk VII 8
    Mk VIII 13, 15
    Special 16, 18, 19
    XJS 60
    XK 120 8, 11, 12, 13, 16, 28, 33
    XK 150 56
Jaguar (Company) 8, 10, 11, 12, 13, 25, 28, 61, 66, 68
James Hardie 1000 60
Jane, Bob 11, 36, 47, 51
Jolly, Derek 42
Jones, Alan 19
Jones, Stan 19, 35
Katoomba 46, 49, 53
Keith-Lucas, Chris (CKL) 64, 66
Le Mans 8, 13, 21, 31, 42, 91
Leaton, George 53
Leaton Motors 38-53
    Racing team 38, 40, 42, 45, 47, 51, 53
Lewis, Ray 15
Leyburn 12, 16
Lister 36

Lola
    1100 48, 49
    Climax 45
Longford 42
    Australian Tourist Trophy 41, 42
Lotus 35
    21 51
    Elite 43, 51
    15 36, 48
    15 40, 42, 43, 45, 46, 47, 49, 51, 53
Lowood 16, 18, 19, 21, 23, 30, 33, 35, 36, 38, 40, 42-43
    Australian Tourist Trophy 36
    Champions Scratch Race 16, 18, 36
    Courier-Mail Tourist Trophy 21, 23, 33
    Queensland Centenary Road Racing Championship 40
    Queensland Road Racing Championship 30, 35
    Queensland Saloon Car Championship 33
    Queensland Tourist Trophy 21, 33, 36
    Sports Car Scratch 42
    Sports and Saloon Car Handicap 18, 35
    Trophy 35, 36
LPS Motors 15
Martin, John 47, 51
Maserati 22, 23, 28, 30, 35, 42, 43
    250F 19, 25, 35
    300S 26, 33, 36, 43, 47, 49, 51

Matich, Frank 35, 36, 38-53, 66
Matich SR3 48
Maybach 30
McKay, David 30, 33, 36, 45, 48, 49
McLaren, Bruce 51
MG 35, 45
    TC Special 59
Mildren, Alec 35, 40, 42
MIRA 10, 66
MobilGas Around Australia Trial (Rally) 13, 15
Modern Motor 21, 48
Mount Druitt 24 Hours 13, 15
Moss, Stirling 22, 23, 25, 26, 31, 36, 46, 51, 63
Murray, Jack 11, 35, 40, 43, 45
National Jaguar Rally 61
Officine Alfieri Maserati 22
Oran Park 54, 59
Parker, Jack 11
Parnell, Reg 22
Patterson, Bill 31, 36
Phillips, Ron 36, 42
Pitt, Bill 12, 13, 15, 16-37, 38, 66
Porsche 35, 45
    Spyder 30
Pritchett special 'Monster' 21
Robinson, Jack 19, 21
Russell, Keith 53, 54, 55, 56
Salvadori, Roy 51
Sandown 51-52, 53, 66
    Kevin Lott Sports Car Trophy 51
Sayer, Malcolm 59, 68, 85, 91

Simca 35
Smith, Reg 45
Spitfire 63
Sports Car World 30
Stahl, Max 48
Standfield, Alan 48, 49, 53, 59
Stillwell, Bib 11, 19, 21, 22, 23, 25, 28, 35, 49, 51
Strathpine 16, 18
Sulman, Tom 26, 43
Surtees, John 51
Swinburne, Charles 13, 15
Topen, Barry 38, 51, 53
Tornado 35
Volkswagen (VW) 13, 15
Warwick Farm 45, 46, 47, 49, 51, 53, 54, 55, 56, 59
    Road Race 46
    Sam Hordern Trophy Race 51
    Sports Car Scratch 51
    Tom Sulman Trophy for Historic Sports and Racing Cars 59
Weber Carburettors 56, 73
Wendt, Eric 33
Westco Motors Pty Ltd 10, 12, 35, 36
Wharton, Ken 22, 23
Whatmore, Charles 16, 18
Whiteford, Doug 26, 28, 35, 36, 43
Whitehead, Peter 13, 15, 22
Whyte, Andrew 13

Bibliography

Sources and abbreviations for their titles where used in the text are as follows:

Magazines and newspapers

Australian Autosportsman (AA)
Australian Jaguar Driver (Jaguar Drivers' Club of Australia)
Australian Motor Sports (AMS)
Jaguar Magazine
Jaguar World Monthly (JWM)
Modern Motor
Motor Manual (MM)
Sports Car World (SCW)
Sydney Morning Herald (SMH)
Wheels

Books

Jaguar D-type - Cars in Profile series – (1973) - John Appleton (aka Andrew Whyte)
Jaguar Under the Southern Cross – (1980) - Les Hughes (JSX)
The Jaguar XK in Australia – (1985) - John Elmgreen and Terry McGrath
Australian Grand Prix – The Official 50-Race History – (1986) - Graham Howard et al
Jaguar Sports Racing & Works Competition Cars From 1954 – Andrew Whyte (1987)
Bathurst – Cradle of Australian Motor Racing – (1997) - John Medley
Glory Days – Albert Park 1953-1958 – (2002) - Barry Green
Historic Racing Cars in Australia – (2004) – John B. Blanden
Norman Dewis of Jaguar – (2006) - Paul Skilleter
Chequered Times – A History of Gnoo Blas – (2012) - Denis Gregory
Jaguar C-type, D-type & Lightweight E-type Register - (2014) – Terry Larson, Penny Woodley, Den Carlow and Paul Skilleter, ed. Anders Ditlev Clausager
Great Cars – Jaguar D-type – The Autobiography of XKD 504 – (2015) – Philip Porter and Chas Parker